Get Set for Philosophy

Douglas Burnham

Edinburgh University Press

© Douglas Burnham, 2003

Edinburgh University Press Ltd
22 George Square, Edinburgh

Typeset in Sabon
by Hewer Text Ltd, Edinburgh, and
printed and bound in Finland by
WS Bookwell

A CIP record for this book is
available from the British Library

ISBN 0 7486 1657 8 (paperback)

CONTENTS

PREFACE

This book is the product of many years of teaching, working with students, talking with colleagues (not *always* in the pub), and reading the many books now available on skills and pedagogy. Several people stand out as having had a more immediate contribution, however: Catherine Burgass, Peter Shott, David Webb and Harvey Young.

INTRODUCTION

If you are reading this, you must be considering (or about to commence) studying philosophy. Philosophy is the most ancient, beautiful and fascinating subject there is – one that is the most likely to make you stand out from the crowd of other graduates and be taken seriously wherever life takes you after university.

Philosophy degrees of one type or another are offered at around fifty universities in the UK, and together these universities take several thousand students each year. And yet, philosophy is not a very common examination subject at schools, even if you include the Religious Studies exams, which have a great deal of philosophy in them. Moreover, philosophy at university will often be quite different in content, style and delivery from study for these examinations. This book aims to bridge such differences. It is aimed at three types of reader:

1. If you are lucky enough to be studying philosophy at school or college, and think you want to go on to university and study for a philosophy degree, then this book will help you to understand the differences between A level and university study. Also, it will help you choose a university.
2. If you are not studying philosophy at school or college, but are fascinated by this subject, then this book will help you to prepare for starting university.
3. If you are about to embark on a university philosophy degree, or have just started one, then this book will help you to orient yourself in the first few months, and polish up your study skills so you can get the most out of your first year.

The book is organised into two parts. Part One is called 'A Guide to Philosophy'. The first section tries to give you a picture of what philosophy study is like at universities in the UK – perhaps this will help you choose which university to attend. The second section is a brief overview of the subject, based again upon how UK universities actually teach the subject, especially in the first year of degree programmes. This section should help you to read the prospectuses sent to you by university departments, to choose any optional courses within your philosophy degree, and to orient your study once you start.

Part Two is called 'Study Skills in Philosophy'. Here you will find helpful advice about all aspects of successful university study, from taking notes to taking exams. We hope that Part Two will be a close companion throughout your university study.

Enjoy!

PART I
A Guide to Philosophy

1 PHILOSOPHY DEGREES

1.1 WHAT IS PHILOSOPHY? WHY STUDY PHILOSOPHY?

1.1.1 What is philosophy?

How do you really irritate a philosopher? Easy: just point to one of those signs that are often put up in shops (pet shops, cosmetics shops, supermarkets, etc.) that say, 'Our philosophy is to always be polite and give our customers excellent service . . .'

Oh, that makes us angry!

Why? Because in such signs, 'philosophy' just means 'policy'; that is, 'the rules we set ourselves in doing business'. Actually, it sometimes doesn't even mean that much; it just means 'opinion'. And, if philosophy just meant 'policy' or 'opinion' there would be no point in worrying about it, studying it, trying to solve problems. Can you imagine a degree at university called 'Opinion Studies'? No, I thought not.

Well, if philosophy doesn't mean 'policy' or 'opinion', what does it mean? Now there's a difficult question! We *could* just answer that philosophy is what philosophers do, what philosophy degrees study, what all the books in the library in the philosophy section are about. But that would not answer the question, because it would not allow us to identify as philosophy a book that had been shelved in the wrong section of the library. Unless we had some idea of what philosophy was, how could we ever put it back into its proper place? No, the question 'What is philosophy?' is asking about what features philosophical enquiry *ought to have* in order to be called philosophy and, more importantly, *why* it ought to have them. We are looking for the *foundations* of philosophy, *any* philosophy at all.

3

Actually, in asking such questions we are already doing philosophy. Philosophers sometimes ask the question 'What is philosophy?' No other subject engages in this self-reflexive activity – or, if they do, it would be a *philosophical line of questioning* quite distinct from the main subject area. In order for a psychologist to ask the question 'Why ought the research I am now doing be considered psychology?', they must pretty much *stop* doing their psychological research, and turn their attention to a different issue altogether. The question being asked is just not a psychological question any longer. Rather it is a question something like: 'What are the *foundations* of psychology such that certain kinds of research (and in particular my current research) ought to be called "Psychology"?' And that is a philosophical question.

This gives us a clue: philosophy frequently has something to do with asking questions of the form 'What are the foundations of X?', where X is a subject of study, like psychology, art, history, physics, medicine, and so on. Let's take another example. Suppose I am a historian, researching some aspect of the English Civil War. How do I know that my research is 'good' history? Well, there are professional standards and no one will publish my book unless I use and interpret my sources according to those standards. But how do I know that those 'standards' are correct and will produce 'good' history? In asking such questions, this is certain: the Civil War has been long forgotten. In fact, these questions are no longer about the past in any sense, and are therefore no longer history. These are philosophical questions about the foundations of the study of history. As a historian, I must assume an answer to this question before I can even *begin* to 'do' history. By 'foundations' we mean the set of ideas, assumptions or practices that are adopted by, say, historians, and can *only be critically examined by philosophers*.

When we asked 'What are the foundations of X?', this X need not be a university-type subject of study. Instead, X could be any activity or way of thinking that is not clearly founded in some other perfectly ordinary activity or way of thinking. So, for example, 'What are the foundations of manufacturing shoes?' is *not* a philosophical question, because the foundations in question are well-known subjects of their own, such as the mechanics of feet and walking, or the chemistry and engineering of rubber or leather. Only when you get to an X that has no obvious foundation, does the question become philosophical. That is why our examples above were university subjects, because studying relatively fundamental disciplines has long been the role of universities. But there are other questions that do not clearly lead to university-type subjects. Two we will discuss briefly below in Chapter 2 are 'What are the foundations of moral behaviour?' and 'What are the foundations of the experience of beauty?' (see pp. 51 and 55 respectively).

For the moment, though, let's go back to the philosophical enquiries into subjects like history or psychology. Are such questions worth asking at all? Many might say it was at best a distraction from the proper business of psychology, history, and so on. Psychologists should just get on with putting rats through mazes; historians should stay in their archives. Others might go so far as to say that the philosophical question is a meaningless enterprise: the question 'What are the foundations of psychology?' has no answer or at least not one that would make the slightest difference to how psychologists work. Nevertheless, these are at least fascinating types of question. Moreover, such questions are in fact asked by many practising physicists, historians and so forth in moments of philosophical reflection. They are also types of question that might, just might, lead to *important and profoundly creative insights into a discipline*. As we have seen, refusing to leave anything unexamined, philosophy even asks such questions of itself.

Not surprisingly, then, you will find courses on your philosophy degree that are called 'The Philosophy of History', 'Medical Ethics', 'The Philosophy of Mind', 'Aesthetics' (which would include the philosophy of art), and so forth. These are courses that examine issues that can only be examined by digging down to the foundations of another subject – something the subject itself cannot do.

Even the more general philosophy courses have this task. 'Epistemology' refers to the philosophy of knowledge. So, a course on 'Epistemology' seeks the foundations of knowledge in general. We are talking about *any* knowledge, now, rather than just psychological or historical types of knowledge. (Of course, it may be that knowledge has no foundation at all. Still, that is an answer to the question of foundation.) Similarly, a course on 'metaphysics' seeks a fundamental understanding of things and their inter-relations – again, *any* things, rather than the particular types of things studied by physicists or historians.

It is not surprising, then, that in the past philosophy was considered the 'Queen' of the sciences: someone who was serious about physics or biology (and who wanted to make fundamental investigations of those subjects) was considered a philosopher. At many ancient universities, the school of natural sciences is called the School of Natural Philosophy, and the highest academic attainment in all such fields is the 'Ph.D.', which stands for Doctor of Philosophy.

1.1.2 Philosophy and your future

You may be a seeker after knowledge and/or you may be going to university for the social life and/or you may be going because it is expected of you. But you've got to pick a subject. Why pick philosophy?

All this questioning, all this not taking anything for granted, makes for certain habits of mind. Philosophers are prized for their clear and penetrating thinking which analyses issues down to their most basic parts; their ability to solve problems creatively by thinking laterally, 'outside the box'; their ability to make and defend arguments, and to head straight for the heart of the mistakes in the arguments of others; their ability to work from the ground up, having the conceptual thoroughness and synthetic organisational abilities that this requires. These are skills that would serve anyone well!

Clearly, philosophy is not a vocational degree in the ordinary sense. Except for those who teach philosophy in schools, colleges and universities, most graduates will not be 'professional philosophers'. But, let's be honest, the same is true of many other subjects: do *all* of the thousands of psychology, film studies, or history graduates (taking three random examples) every year actually become practising professional psychologists, film-makers or historians? Of course not. A few do (often very few) but the others study the subject because they like it, and because studying *anything* at university is good. But like no other subject, philosophy does equip its students with the tools to succeed in a wide variety of vocations. The above 'habits of mind' are valued by employers in most professions: from business to law, from journalism to public service. In any such profession, your employer will want to train you in certain skills that are particular to that job, but the philosophy graduate will have, let us say, a 'ready-made' working brain, able to acquire these skills, and, what is more, able to see, analyse and solve problems. A degree in philosophy doesn't limit you, it removes limits, allowing you to master anything to which you set your mind. In today's global, mobile economy, what could be more important?

These same habits of mind are also socially important: a philosopher is best equipped to see through the cloudy reasoning and rhetorical ploys of those in positions of power. A philosopher can thus become the best kind of citizen in an extraordinarily complex, information-rich world. Finally, and most importantly, philosophy is a life-long passion. You don't need a laboratory or a vast archive to carry on with philosophy after you graduate, just a few books and some time to think. The subject will continue to enrich your life for decades to come; philosophy can help you grow, and carry on growing, as a person. You may find few answers to your questions, but you will discover and learn to use the tools needed to evaluate possible answers!

In addition to the above philosophical skills that you will leave university with because of with your philosophy degree, there are also what are frequently called 'transferable skills'.

These are the skills that any university subject will teach. These too are important for your personal development, and your job prospects, and you have to make sure your prospective employer knows you have them.

General transferable skills
- University graduates are self-motivating.

- They are good at time management.

- They can work under pressure.

- They can meet deadlines.

- They have learned from their tutorials how to be team-players, how to work as part of a group.

- They have shown that they are well-rounded individuals by taking an active part in at least one of the sporting, social or intellectual activities offered by university societies or clubs.

These skills are the reason why university graduates tend to get jobs more readily, earn more on average, and advance to positions of greater influence more quickly. So, a university degree is an excellent move in general, and a philosophy degree is an excellent way of making that move.

1.1.3 A special word to mature students

Some mature students worry too much. Certainly, if you are a mature student coming to university for the first time, you may have many problems to contend with that students straight from school do not have. You may have family commitments, young children and all the worries about childcare that parenthood entails. However, your university may provide good-quality, low-cost childcare. This is worth finding out about. You may have got out of the habit of studying, writing essays and sitting exams, and the young students seem incredibly self-confident and knowledgeable.

However, you will soon get back into the way of studying and you would not have been admitted to university if you did not have the ability to succeed, so there is no reason to compare your talents unfavourably with those of younger students. For some reason, many mature students feel that they have to do *better* than the younger students to prove to themselves that they can do as well. If this sounds like you, calm down. Your maturity gives you extra skills, particularly in time management and communication. It is always a joy to teach mature students because of their high level of motivation and because they ask lots of questions. If any domestic crises should occur, or if you are having difficulty with any aspect of study, you will find that members of staff are very understanding and supportive.

In short, mature students are no longer just 'different' from 'ordinary' students. You are at university by right, based upon your ability, and you have a lot to offer!

1.2 PHILOSOPHY AT UNIVERSITY

In choosing where to study philosophy, you basically have two decisions to make: which university (and thus which philosophy department), and which type of degree?

1.2.1 Choosing where to study: which university?

Now, there are plenty of books around to help you decide on the university. They tell you how inexpensive an area is to live, how active the Student Union is, how friendly the atmosphere is, and so forth. Covering this ground again is not our purpose here. Similarly, we cannot here discuss the differences in university structure and funding between England, Wales, Northern Ireland and Scotland, or between the ancient and the newer universities. The following brief account only speaks of those things that matter to your philosophy degree, and touches upon issues that commonly arise at UK universities.

In choosing a university, there are only four things that matter:

1. Whether you would enjoy being there. Well, you may as well have fun with these few years, but there is a much more important angle. If you enjoy it (the university but above all the degree course), that enjoyment will get you through the times of hard slog, and it will motivate you to study with greater energy, and thus get better marks. Those better marks can have long-term consequences! However, it is worth remembering that *all* universities have Student Unions with live bands, plenty of special-interest organisations and sports facilities, are surrounded by friendly pubs, and are no more than a bus ride from shops, restaurants, clubs and so forth. Honestly, if you allow yourself, you are likely to enjoy yourself pretty much anywhere. Thus, our advice is to look carefully at the particular philosophy department within the university.

2. Whether you can afford to go there. This may be more serious, because some areas are considerably more expensive to live in than others, and it may not be long before some universities will charge higher fees than others. On the other hand, never in your life will you have a cheaper loan than a student loan.

3. The prestige of the university. This really only matters after you graduate, but it remains the case that a degree from a prestigious university can open a few extra employment doors for you. Of course, the entrance requirements are likely to be higher, and often the living costs too. Furthermore, as we shall see below, it is important to remember that you are studying in a particular department, and for the most part the rest of the university will rarely impinge upon your life.

4. Above all, whether the philosophy department is the place you want to study.

Any university is a big institution, with a thousand or more employees working in dozens of buildings, and offering many different degrees and combinations. Because of this, deciding where to study philosophy only by looking at the university would be like deciding to buy a house based entirely upon what county it is in! If you are studying philosophy some-where, will it matter that much to you if the engineering department is well regarded, or the chemistry faculty is wealthy, and so forth? Similarly, the 'league tables' published in the national press tend to lump all the various departments, institutions and activities of a university together, weighting various factors in arbitrary ways. Accordingly, they are not really terribly useful. When using such tables, keep your eyes open: how are the various factors weighted to reach an overall score – do these weightings reflect what you feel is important? Are some of the factors even relevant to your study? Are the tables about the Philosophy department, or about the uni-versity as a whole? And if the latter, how valuable are they as a guide? In general, there is no university in the country that is not worth studying at; similarly, there is no university that will turn you into a genius or a millionaire just by your being there.

So, at least as important as the university is the actual department that offers your degree. By 'department' is meant the group of individuals who, for the most part, provide and manage the elements of your degree programme – that is, the philosophers. We should note that not all universities call their academic sub-units 'departments', but we will use this word for convenience. Frequently too there will be an intermediate grouping of individuals and subjects, called a 'School', 'Col-lege' or 'Faculty'. The philosophy department at some uni-versities is in the School of Humanities, at others in the School of Social Sciences. Occasionally, philosophy is within a larger department of politics perhaps, or theology. *What counts are the award you are studying for, the courses you take and the group of philosophers you work with*. The administrative organisation of the place will bear little significance to your decision.

The reason why looking at the department is so important is

that every department does things differently. For example, the staff at some departments may all specialise in one or two sub-types of philosophy. From your A level study, or from your reading around the subject, you may already have a sense of which kind of philosophy you wish to study. So you should find out if a given department even offers it, or if it is offered only as a token with respect to other topics in which you have much less interest. Again, some departments emphasise examinations over coursework, or vice versa – and you may have good reasons for feeling that one or the other is advantageous to you. The university will have a big prospectus, describing all its offerings, and this will give you some information about the department. However, for much more information, the department may also have its own, specialised information packs, and normally will maintain a website. You can go and visit on pre-scheduled 'open days', and you should also feel free to contact someone in the department. The prospectus will give you a telephone number or email address.

In evaluating departments, you might wish to consider some or all of the following:

- Specialisms: do the courses on offer sound like subjects you would be interested in? Similarly, have a look at the list of staff members and their interests. These interests will inevitably come across in the teaching.

- Examinations/coursework: don't forget also to look at how courses are assessed in the second, third (and fourth) years. You may have good reasons for trying to avoid examinations, or alternatively for limiting the number of essays you are required to write.

- Postgraduate awards: does the department have an interesting looking MA degree, and does it have any research students? Named MA awards are also a good way of quickly establishing the specialism(s) of a department. Postgraduates are interesting and enthusiastic individuals that can enliven the general atmosphere of the department, and raise the level of debate in the common room or pub. Having such postgraduate programmes can also be a sign of a department that has some kudos in its areas of specialisation.

- On the other hand, enquire after who your tutors will be. Does the department often utilise postgraduate (sometimes even advanced undergraduate) students for teaching, or are you face to face with members of staff most of the time? Postgraduates can be more enthusiastic teachers, or you may feel more comfortable with the greater experience and expertise of the permanent members of staff.

- Choice: do you have any choice in the various courses that make up your degree; can you choose to 'customise' your degree by emphasising certain topics? Have a look at the section 'Which type of degree?' below, which talks about how degrees tend to be structured.

- Teaching: Ask what a typical week would be like for you: how many big lectures; when are classes scheduled; how many small-group discussions and how small are they; how often do you get to speak with a tutor one-on-one? You may have strong opinions about what type of teaching suits you. For some strange reason, students tend to like big lectures, but this is often not the best way of 'doing' philosophy.

- Quality Assurance Agency (QAA) Score: all philosophy departments have recently been assessed as to the overall quality of their degree programmes. The assessment concerned such issues as whether courses were well structured, well taught, and appropriately assessed; whether the department and university provided adequate support and resources (such as libraries); whether students were kept well informed and had a say in how things were run; and whether the department had procedures in place to monitor and maintain its own quality. Most philosophy departments received an 'excellent' rating in this procedure, so no matter where you go you are likely to receive a top-quality education. For the next inspections, the system changes and the top rating is 'Commendable.'

- Research Assessment Exercise (RAE) Score: this is a measurement (on the rather cumbersome scale: 1, 2, 3b, 31, 4, 5, 5*) of the importance of a department as a research establishment. For an undergraduate degree, this is not terribly important. As long as the department has *some* research production, you can be sure that your tutors are active in their fields, and thus the education you receive will be current and well informed. Indeed, watch out for high-flying staff in the top-rated departments being off on research leave (or, assigned to postgraduate education only). You might not see them for two or more years, and the book they are writing will not appear until after you graduate. They may as well work at a university on Mars for all the good it does you. A high research rating is more important for postgraduate education, clearly.

- Size: some departments have only two or three members of teaching staff, others have a dozen or more. (Note that staff who are labelled 'Research' may have no teaching duties, and thus you may never see them.) The number of students will be roughly proportional. It might be important to you to study in a small department where you know everyone, and everyone knows you, and it's easy to get to see a tutor when you need to. In smaller departments, your classes may be smaller and more informal as well. Or, you might like working in a larger place, where there is more variety and hundreds of people to meet.

Most prospective students, then, will probably be better off choosing the department first, and the university only second. Sadly, this is exactly the reverse of how these choices are usually made.

1.2.2 Which type of degree?

The other decision you have to make concerns your degree. To understand what this means, we need to talk about how universities typically put degrees together.

First of all, you will have to choose between a single-honours degree and a joint-honours degree. The basic difference is easy enough: on a single-honours award, you study pretty much only philosophy; on a joint-honours award, you study philosophy and one other subject (so, for example, a BA (Hons) in Philosophy and Psychology). We'll return to the single/joint decision below; let's look now at the various courses that make up such awards.

In general, degrees are made up of several types of 'course' or 'module'. Many universities employ a 'credits' system (called Credit Accumulation and Transfer Scheme (CATS)). Each course carries a certain number of credits (typically 10, 15, or 20). For example, you may be required to take and pass 120 credits in your first year, and in each year thereafter, ending (if the award is three years long) with 360 credits.

First, there are 'core' or 'required' courses. Obviously enough, these are courses you have to take as part of your philosophy degree, whether it is single or joint. The staff feel that these courses will help you to understand what you need in order to do well on other philosophy courses. So, such courses may provide an overall survey of philosophy (especially in the first year), helping you to orient yourself in the subject; and they may also help you to acquire general philosophical skills (critical reasoning, essay writing, whatever). You will frequently be required to undertake an extended research project (often called a 'dissertation') in your final year. This involves you working much more independently, researching a topic of your choice, and then writing an essay of a length that will probably seem inconceivable to you now! Most students find this is one of the most rewarding parts of their study, though, and no matter how frightening the word length seems at first, it never seems to be enough.

Second, there are 'distribution' courses. In this case you may be required to take one of two or more courses, but you can choose which one. For example, your degree may require that you study some ethics, but you can choose which of several courses on ethics you take to fulfil this requirement. You should be aware that sometimes such courses are designed to link together end-to-end. To take an obvious example, you may have to take a course entitled 'Introduction to X' as a 'prerequisite' for taking 'Advanced X'.

Third, there are 'optional' courses. In this case your choice is freer. You need to take a certain number of courses (or a certain number of 'credits') in order to graduate; for example, you may need 90 credits of philosophy courses in your first year. But, after the core courses are out of the way, it may be that the courses you take to accumulate the necessary total is pretty much up to you. These courses may also be linked together by a 'prerequisite' structure.

Fourth, you may be allowed the freedom to take one or two completely free 'electives'. These courses may not even be in the philosophy department, and may not even be directly related to philosophy – but are there to allow you to pick up extra skills you may want, or just to satisfy a curiosity for a different subject. For example, there may be courses in languages, or in cv writing and preparing for job interviews.

All of the above are usually further differentiated by level. A first-year course is designed for new students; a second- or third-year/level course is designed for students with some experience behind them. Normally, you will be required to take only first-year courses in your first year, and mostly higher level courses thereafter. So, as you move from the first to the second year, you will find a completely new selection of core and optional courses.

Single and joint honours degrees will have a certain structure made up of some or all of the above types. A degree in philosophy alone (a single-honours degree) means your award is in only the one subject. You'll pretty much take philosophy courses all the way through. (In your first year, however, there may be a requirement to take a 'supplementary' subject: introductory courses from a different discipline to help ensure your education is reasonably rounded. You may also have a few free choice courses.) You will almost certainly be required to do a final-year dissertation: an extended and largely independently research project, on a philosophical topic of particular interest to you. For this reason, single-honours awards can have greater focus and depth to them. However, much depends upon the design of the award. If it's just a matter of taking a bunch of courses in the areas that staff happen to be interested in, these may not build one upon another or in other ways relate to each other. This is not very common any more but, in such cases, depth and focus may be lacking.

The following are typical examples of the manner in which some departments try to build a fully coherent programme of study: the ability to return in a later year and at greater depth to a subject encountered in the first year (e.g. Plato); the building of some courses into definite sequences (sometimes unimaginatively titled: e.g. Epistemology I, followed by Epistemology II); or themes running through the award (e.g. applied ethics, the philosophy of language, European philosophy).

Alternatively, you can study for a joint-honours degree, which combines with a philosophy curriculum that of another subject. In terms of the structure of that degree, it will look like two down-sized single-honours degree side by side. For example, there may be two different sets of core courses, and two different (but probably smaller) sets of distribution and optional courses.

If you think about the way we defined philosophy above, you'll see that philosophy makes an ideal subject to study alongside another. You won't spend as much time studying either subject as you would a single-honours programme, but joint-honours degrees are just as serious and reputable as single honours degrees, and are not an 'easy' option. Such degrees tend to suit students who have a wider range of interests, or who have a particular interest in the philosophical aspects of another subject. Excellent combinations frequently found include philosophy and:

- English (or Literature);

- Politics;

- Psychology;

- History;

- Sociology;

- Classics or a Classical Language, French or German; and

- Computing/Artificial Intelligence.

But many other combinations are possible and worthy. Each university will be very clear about the combinations it offers.

At a few universities, it is possible to study three subjects: one relatively rare but historically very distinguished such combination is PPE: Philosophy, Politics and Economics. Also, at some universities you can *begin* studying several subjects (e.g. philosophy, English and psychology), but not continuing with all of them through three years. This provides an introduction to several disciplines, but a focus on one. Such an arrangement is sometimes called a 'combined-honours degree'. If you are unsure about which subjects might be for you, this is an excellent route – again, it is not an 'easy' option, and might even be slightly more difficult during that first year, having to come to terms with three subjects and three departments. Note that you are also less likely to have much real choice in which courses you take: with three subjects (and probably three sets of core courses) your timetable will be quite packed, though of course you will have already exercised considerable choice in choosing the three subjects!

Above, we said that, structurally, a joint-honours degree (or one of the variations just discussed) tends to be like two slightly reduced single-honours degrees side-by-side. Indeed, some combinations, offered by some universities, are just two half degrees arbitrarily stuck together. There is nothing wrong with this, but there may be little opportunity (outside of your own head!) to relate the one subject to the other. Since philosophy is so concerned with understanding disciplinary foundations, this is a pity. However, other universities really make an effort to offer courses that bring the two subjects together. For example, on a philosophy and literature joint-honours programme, you might find some courses that deal with the philosophy of literature, or 'literary' philosophy. In other words, although the joint-honours degree structure is in two halves, it doesn't necessarily mean that the departments do not make an effort to help you to 'unify' your degree. If you are considering a joint-honours degree, you might wish to turn your attention to universities that offer such genuine 'inter-disciplinary' opportunities.

1.2.3 Typical philosophy courses

In this section, we'll be talking about the kinds of individual course you are likely to come across within your philosophy degree. There are two ways we can divide courses up: in terms of the way a subject is taught, and the subject matter itself.

There are essentially four ways in which philosophy courses are taught: survey, historical, problem and text.

- Survey: this type of course will attempt to provide a broad overview of a philosophical issue. A course on 'Epistemology', for example, might start with an excerpt from Plato, an ancient Greek philosopher. You spend a week or two thinking about and evaluating what Plato has to say, perhaps also reading recent philosophers who write about Plato. Then, you might move on to a medieval philosopher, and then to more modern philosophers such as Descartes or Hume, before finishing off with a couple of twentieth- and twenty-first-century philosophers. The idea is to introduce a variety of ways of tackling a philosophical issue, each of which seems to have its strengths and weaknesses. This approach is typical of introductory-level courses and core courses, because it is good for providing a sense of the history of philosophy, the way that philosophy has developed, and it is obviously a good manner of helping students to grasp some basic ideas and vocabulary.

- Historical: similar to a survey course, but with a narrower historical scope, and often with a wider conceptual content. A course entitled 'Ancient Greek Philosophy' would be an example. The epistemology course described above covered many centuries, but always on the one issue. Now, 'Ancient Greek Philosophy' might cover only a few decades of the fourth century BC, but wander from epistemology, to ethics and politics, and on to metaphysics. Such a course tries to introduce and explore the kind of thinking typical of a certain epoch, increasing the depth of your knowledge of the history of philosophy, and also showing how ideas or arguments from different types of philosophy can influence one another. How does Plato's philosophy of knowledge, for example, relate to his treatment of ethics? (Notice that the ancient Greek course also has geographical limits, according to the plausible idea that people who share a culture and might even know each other might also have ideas that relate together.)

- Problem: a problem-based course will not necessarily have a historical angle at all, but will start with an issue or question, and draw on whatever resources are needed to explore it. For example, a course on medical ethics will pose a series of important moral issues (e.g. should euthanasia be permitted? Or what would be a just way of dividing up limited health-care resources?) and then turn to philosophers of any period for help in introducing or clarifying concepts, and supplying arguments. In our example of medical ethics, most of the philosophers consulted will be relatively recent, since such moral problems are more often studied in recent philosophy. But one should not discount the possibility that a philosopher from centuries past might have something important to say about life, death or justice! In any case, the purpose of such a course is to show how particular issues can be addressed from a variety of directions, and perhaps to propose and evaluate solutions to contemporary problems.

- Text: a text-based course will work its way slowly through a particular text by a particular philosopher. For example, a course on Plato might read all or most of the *Republic*. Such a course will expect you to come to grips with the detail of the book, and something of the way key passages have been interpreted, argued for, or argued against, by philosophers after Plato. Sometimes, a text-based course may ask you to read two or three texts by a given philosopher. The purpose of the text-based course is to allow you to deal with the *system* of a philosopher, the way his or her various ideas (across several areas of philosophy) influence, reinforce and deepen one another. This is an exhilarating experience, and one you cannot really have on any of the other types of courses.

Obviously, there will be many courses of a mixed type. For example, a course on ancient Greek philosophy might require patiently reading a few books in their entirety, thus mixing the historical and text-based types. Or a survey course can take as its organising theme not a broad topic (such as epistemology) but a particular problem (what is science?).

Notice that for each of the above types, there is given a suggestion of its 'purpose'. Your tutors will tend to design their courses *backwards*, from the point of view of the *outcome*. That is, they will ask 'What is it that my students will want to, or need to, get out of this course?' or 'What do I expect that their assessments (essays, exams, etc.) will show my students can do?' The course (both the content and perhaps also even the *way* it is taught) will then be constructed so as to enable you to achieve those outcomes. Your lecturers do not just get up in the morning and say to themselves 'I think I'll give a lecture on Descartes today' – instead, every activity on the course is oriented in advance to these broad purposes or outcomes. When it comes to studying for these courses, and writing essays or examinations for them, it will help to have some sense of how your tutors design courses backwards, as it were, from their educational purpose.

2 AN ORIENTATION IN PHILOSOPHY

2.1 INTRODUCTION

There are many tools to help you in your study of philosophy. In your library, and on the Internet, you will find huge encyclopedias of philosophy. No student should go without buying a good dictionary of philosophy to have by his or her side. There are many excellent introductions to philosophy in print, and naturally your courses at university will set out to introduce philosophy to you. So, what can we do in this section that isn't done better, elsewhere?

The aim here is to help you orient yourself in philosophy as it is taught at UK universities. This will involve sketching out each of the main areas of philosophy in terms of some of the key topics and figures typically encountered by first-year university students. Each sketch will be very brief, because its purpose is not to tell you about philosophy – not, that is, to introduce philosophy as such – but to tell you about philosophy *courses* and *degrees*. For the same reason, you would be ill-advised to use the following as a secondary source for an essay! You will also find a conceptual map of philosophy and a timeline.

Distributed through this chapter you will come across brief entries on philosophers you are likely to encounter on your first year.

2.1.1 A note on sample essays and examination answers

You will also find below a couple of sample essays, examination answers and presentation scripts, each with a commentary. Ignore the commentary for the moment, since it will make most sense with respect to the advice on essay and exam writing in Part Two of this book. There is a mind-map for an essay on Descartes, and a sample examination paper, in Part Two of this book.

Descartes, René (1596–1650) Descartes is one of those figures in the history of philosophy who is so famous as to often stand for philosophy itself. This fame has a great deal to do with the extravagance of his 'method of doubt' (in which Descartes set out to discover truth by first eliminating everything of which there could be the slightest doubt), and his 'I think therefore I am' (which is the moment at which Descartes discovers the one thing that is beyond doubt: his own existence). These are key moments in Descartes, to be sure, but there is much more to his work. In these famous moments, he appears to take a first-person point of view and tries to describe a mind coming to understand itself and know the world around it. Oddly, this approach was influential for philosophers who disagreed with virtually everything Descartes said (the empiricist tradition in the seventeenth and eighteenth centuries), but it was for the most part ignored by philosophers who might have considered themselves as working in the tradition of Descartes (the series of philosophers often called the 'rationalists', such as Spinoza or Leibniz). This is an object lesson to philosophers in their first years of study: any philosopher of significance is going to be (in themselves and in their influence) more complex, more sophisticated and ultimately much more interesting than a couple of ideas taken in isolation would lead you to believe.

The aim in providing these samples is:

- To give you examples of each of the key types of work you will be asked to do in your first year at university. Not only are there samples of essays, exams and presentations, but also the examples represent work for different kinds of courses. For example, the sample essay on Plato would be for a text-based course; whereas the presentation about abstract ideas would be for a problem course.

- To provide you with samples of how to move from essay or exam questions, to answers. You will find extended advice on how to analyse questions in Part Two below.

- To give you models of good work, certainly – but not *perfect* work. All of the samples below have weaknesses, because you will need to be able recognise weaknesses and remedy them. The commentaries point out and discuss the weaknesses. But are there some additional problems you can see?

- To give you some examples of a good referencing style. (It should be pointed out, however, that most of the references are fictional. My hope is that this will serve as a reminder that these texts are meant to be representations of student work, and not secondary sources!) For a full discussion of referencing, see Part Two.

2.1.2 Books

Introductions to philosophy come in many varieties and tones. My recommendation is to spend some money on good reference texts (see below), but let your first-year courses be your introduction to the subject. And, indeed, those courses may well require you to purchase introductory books; if you are a month or two away from starting university, contact the department for advice about required texts for your first semester.

Every philosophy student needs a dictionary of philosophy. Those from Oxford, Penguin and Cambridge are all good – choose the one that 'reads' well to you after an extended browse. Also, have a look at the *Oxford Companion to Philosophy*, and the *Concise Routledge Encyclopaedia of Philosophy* (your university Library may hold the full Routledge encyclopedia, or a web-licence for their students to use it).

On individual areas of philosophy, or individual philosophers, you'll find Routledge Guides, Cambridge Companions, and Blackwell Dictionaries. Edinburgh University Press will soon commence publishing a new series of this type. Oxford University Press also publishes two volumes of extended essays on major areas and philosophers: *Philosophy 1* and *Philosophy 2*.

Hume, David (1711–76) Working largely in the empiricist tradition of Locke, Hume's philosophy was nevertheless significantly different in many of its conclusions. Hume explores the implications of his assumption that the only positive data the mind has to work with are immediate sensations, and thus that no idea about ourselves, the world or even God can have any validity unless it can be, and to the extent that it can be, traced back to that data. Hume is particularly famous for his sceptical conclusions concerning metaphysics. For example, he argues that not only do we have no way of demonstrating with certainty that one thing causes another, but that our concept of causation is, strictly speaking, empty nonsense, since observation of a cause is never part of the above positive data. The task of philosophy is less to acquire knowledge than to examine carefully the psychological reasons that we believe we have knowledge. A similar procedure is applied to ethics: what are the psychological operations behind the use of words such as 'good' or 'virtue'. Hume made important contributions to (among others) aesthetics and political philosophy, and had an enormous influence on a wide variety of subsequent philosophers, such as Adam Smith, the utilitarians and Kant.

Several publishers produce series of tiny, brief books about major philosophers. These can be entertainingly written, but are not usually produced for university students, and thus normally should be avoided.

On the Internet you will find two encyclopedias of philosophy, neither yet complete, but already containing much that you will find useful: the Internet Encyclopedia of Philosophy and the Stanford Encyclopedia. The Internet is groaning with introductory material, some of it excellent, some not. You need to be very careful. Don't let a professional-looking site fool you into thinking that the philosophy it contains is equally professional. Check the origin of everything you find.

2.2 TYPICAL COURSES ON THE FIRST YEAR OF PHILOSOPHY DEGREES

In terms of the subject matter of philosophy courses, there is no end of possibilities. Any philosopher from the past, any historical period, any problem upon which philosophy can be brought to bear, any other academic discipline, all can form the subject matter of a philosophy course. However, it is not difficult to predict which course you are *most likely* to come across, especially in your first year. A survey of UK universities reveals that the following are very common:

1. Problems of metaphysics.
2. Epistemology and philosophy of science.
3. Ethics, applied ethics and political philosophy.
4. Aesthetics.
5. The philosophy of religion.
6. Ancient philosophy.
7. Early modern philosophy.
8. 'European' philosophy.
9. Logic.
10. Specialist and interdisciplinary courses.

Most of the above receive comment below. The ninth is missing because an introduction to logic as a tool for the analysis of arguments is given in the Part Two of this book. Furthermore, Philosophical Logic (that is, logic not so much as a tool but as the subject matter of philosophical enquiry) is only rarely encountered as a course in the first year, although issues do pop up in introductory survey courses, where you may come across titbits of Frege or Russell. The tenth, too, is missing, but that is because it is a catch-all category. Sometimes, philosophy departments can be very creative in what they offer their first-year students, and offer very particular courses rarely found elsewhere, which may indeed reflect a research interest in the department. Examples include Scottish philosophy, or a philosophical history of cosmology. Similarly, departments may offer courses that provide genuine interdisciplinary study for joint-honours awards, such as a course in philosophy and literature.

Figure 2.1 is a kind of map to some of the key sub-topics in philosophy. It is a rather crude map, both because it leaves out some important subjects, and also because it simplifies relationships. A few examples: it seems to imply that 'The philosophy of mind' has nothing to do with 'epistemology'; that 'logic' has nothing to do with science; and that 'ontology' is on its own at the bottom of the tree. All of these are just false. However, as an aide to help you get oriented in philosophy, it should help.

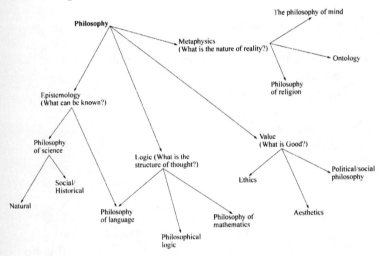

Figure 2.1   A map of philosophy

Figure 2.2 lays things out in time, in the conventional form of a timeline of names and events. Again, there are simplifications: the dates are all approximate, many figures have been left out, and the focus is on Western philosophy. The philosophers you are most likely to come across in your first year are in the first column after the dates. Scientists and artists tend to be over on the right-hand columns.

Kant, Immanuel (1724–1804) One of the most important philosophers of the eighteenth century, or of any century, Kant revolutionised the philosophy that came after him. One of his most distinctive contributions was the 'transcendental' method, which tries to establish the most fundamental conditions under which any experience is possible. In epistemology, this involved demonstrating the universal validity of a set of categories, and that space and time are the 'form' of our relationship to things, and not part of the content of that relation. Similarly, in the field of ethics, Kant tries to show that ethics is only possible as action in accordance with duty as prescribed by reason – and he then sets out to describe the laws of moral duty on the basis of reason. Kant is also known as a 'critical' philosopher, whose work is constantly trying to show that certain forms of philosophy (for example, metaphysical studies of the nature of the soul) have only a limited validity and that outside these limits are meaningless. (Thus Kant's chief works are the three 'Critiques', beginning with the 'Critique of Pure Reason', first published in 1781.) Kant made important contributions to epistemology, metaphysics, ethics and aesthetics, among others. Kant was influenced especially by Leibniz, Rousseau and Hume, and he was very influential in turn on German Idealism.

2.2.1 Problems of metaphysics

A grand name, with an apparently pedestrian origin. For many centuries, in compiling works by the ancient Greek philosopher Aristotle, it was customary for the works on physics to be put together, followed by some other works that were not on physics. The subject matter of these other works came to have the label 'metaphysics', which simply means, roughly, 'the texts that come after the texts on physics'.

However, the name 'metaphysics' is not completely arbitrary (nor was the edited order of Aristotle's works) because the subject matter of metaphysics consisted of topics that fell

Selected Political and Social References	Date				
First Olympic Games	800				Homer
	700			Hesiod	
	600		Anaximander, Anaximenes	Thales	
'Golden Age' of Greece / Hellenic Age	500	Socrates	Heraclitus/ Parmenides, Zeno/Protagoras	Pythagoras, Anaxagoras, Democritus	Sophocles
	400	Plato, Aristotle	Diogenes of Sinope		
Alexander the Great / Hellenistic Age	300		Epicurus/Zeno of Citium, Arcesilaus	Pyrrho of Elis/Euclid, Aristarchus of Samos/Archimedes	
	200			Eratosthenes	
Roman Period	100		Lucretius	Cicero	
	0		Jesus, Aenesidemus/St Paul		
Romans invade Britain	100		Marcus Aurelius	Seneca, Ptolemy	
	200		Plotinus	Origen	
Christianisation of Rome	300	Augustine			
	400		Proclus		

Date	Events	Philosophers		
500	Fall of the Roman Empire in the West	Boethius		
600		Muhammad		
700	Rise of Islamic scholarship		Isidore of Seville	
800	Charlemagne and Carolingian Renaissance / Holy Roman Empire	Al-Kindi / Al-Farabi		
900	Founding of the University of Cordoba			
1000		Avicenna		
1100	Schism of Rome with Byzantium	St Anselm		
1200	Crusades begin / University of Paris / Gothic Period / Introduction of Islamic learning into Western Europe / Founding of Christian universities	Averoës / Maimonides / St Aquinas		
1300	Oxford University	Duns Scotus		Dante
1400	Italian 'Renaissance'	Nicolas of Cusa		Chaucer

Events	Date				Arts
Fall of Byzantium/ printing press			Ficino/ Mirandola		Leonardo da Vinci
Circumnavigation of the Globe	1500		Copernicus	Luther	Michelangelo
Reformation and 'modern' period				Calvin	Shakespeare
English Civil War	1600	Bacon/ Hobbes Descartes	Spinoza Leibniz	Galileo/Kepler/Newton	Milton
	1700	Locke Berkeley/Hume/ Kant			Bach
Industrial Revolution			Smith/Bentham/Reid	Herschel	Goethe Wordsworth
French Revolution	1800	Mill	Hegel/Laplace/Gauss/ Darwin	Mozart/Beethoven	Dickens/ Wagner/ Brahms
Napoleonic Wars		Marx/James/ Nietzsche	Schopenhauer/Emerson Kierkegaard/Comte Pierce	Kelvin/Maxwell	Cezanne/ Picasso
Russian Revolution/WWI	1900	Russell	Frege/Husserl/Bergson/ Freud	Einstein/Bohr	Schonberg/ Stravinski
WW II		Wittgenstein/ Sartre/Ayer/ Ryle	Heidegger/Quine/ Adorno/Rawls	T. S.Eliot/Joyce	

Figure 2.2   Timeline of Western philosophy

Nietzsche, Friedrich (1844–1900) Nietzsche had very little influence during his lifetime, but by the turn of the century was becoming a 'must-read' for intellectuals right across Europe. Nietzsche's work often takes the form of brief, apparently disconnected 'fragments', in which he makes frequent use of irony, parody and hyperbole. For this reason, Nietzsche should not be read simply as a traditional philosophical writer. (With little sensitivity for his style, Nietzsche can appear to be, among many other things, wildly anti-Semitic. He was thus wrongly hailed as a pioneer by the Nazis.) Throughout his life, Nietzsche was concerned above all with what he often called the 'health' of an individual and of culture more generally. By 'health' he meant, roughly, that thought and expression is in direct accord with the innermost drives of the individual or his or her culture. Accordingly, Nietzsche diagnoses many aspects of modern life – its scientific, economic, or artistic preoccupations, its metaphysical assumptions, but above all its understanding of ethics – as symptoms of a lack of health, in other words of the repression, misunderstanding or misdirection of such drives. Nietzsche was influenced by Schopenhauer and by aspects of nineteenth-century science, especially Darwin (although he professed considerable disagreement with both). His influence was perhaps most important in twentieth-century art and literature, but also on Freud and existentialism.

outside the remit of physics, but were nonetheless closely related to physics. For example, while physicists might concern themselves with types of material and their behaviour under certain conditions, metaphysics might concern itself with the questions 'What, in general, is *substance*? Where does it come from? How can it be created, or destroyed?' Or, another example, while physicists might study how things move in space, or how the spatial shapes of things come about (crystals, for example), a metaphysician would ask, 'What, exactly, is motion as such? And what kind of a thing is space?'

This takes us back to our definition of philosophy. You can

easily see from the above how physical and metaphysical questions are linked, but are not by any means the same. But, more than this, you can see how the metaphysical questions are outside the remit of physics, such that a physicist who asked metaphysical questions would have to stop being a physicist. But it's not just physics strictly speaking that metaphysics has this curious relationship to. Similar things can be said of biology, psychology, mathematics, and so on. This is perhaps where the common assumption arises that metaphysics deals with more 'fundamental' or 'deep' questions. However, it can certainly be argued that such questions are trivial or even meaningless, and that the real business of human thought takes place in those sciences, and nowhere else. The question of whether metaphysics is possible at all, or is not rather an empty and fruitless endeavour, might well pop up in your first-year metaphysics course. It will certainly pop up in later years if you study (for example) Hume, Kant, Nietzsche or positivism.

However, let us assume that metaphysics does have this 'fundamental' relationship to the sciences. Then, we can define metaphysics as that branch of philosophy that deals with the nature of various types of existence, and of existence in general, such that any given field of knowledge has an object that it can study. Accordingly, metaphysics almost always includes the study of 'ontology', which simply means the study of being or existence itself. Not all metaphysical questions are necessarily ontological: if I were to ask the above question 'What kind of a thing is space?' I am already assuming that space is 'a thing', and thus the ontological question of whether space 'is' at all, has been bypassed.

It is important also to see that there might be a link between metaphysics and epistemology (the study of knowledge). To the extent that I can have knowledge of things that exist, I must already be able to characterise what existence as such is. For example, for me to be able to say what the properties of 'calcium' are, I must already know what it means for a thing to be and to 'have' properties. Following this line of argument, metaphysics is not only fundamental with respect to, say,

Positivism A mainly nineteenth-century trend in philosophy, found most clearly in the French philosopher Comte, and in a modified form in Mill. A key claim is that all knowledge is within the boundaries of the empirical sciences. This means that the boundaries of the sciences need to be clearly mapped out, and positivism is thus characterised by a concern with the philosophy of science. But it also means that if metaphysics, as traditionally practised, concerns claims that are not empirical or scientific in character, then metaphysics has to be excluded from the field of knowledge. Positivists were influenced by seventeenth- and eighteenth-century empiricism (Locke and Hume especially), but also by the 'critical' philosophy of Kant. Positivism has had an important influence on twentieth-century philosophy of science. Although overlapping and historically related, positivism should not be confused with the 'logical positivism' of the early twentieth century, the representative of which you are most likely to encounter is A. J. Ayer.

physics, but fundamental as well for other important areas of philosophical enquiry. Still, we need to make a distinction. On the one hand, there is 'metaphysics' in the sense of 'that which is assumed by any body of knowledge' – in the above example, what is assumed is 'what it means for a thing to be and to "have" properties'. We might call this first sense 'metaphysical knowledge'. And, on the other hand, a different sense of metaphysics, which is 'a characterisation of the objects that are known independently of our knowledge of them'. Such metaphysics tries as hard as possible to avoid epistemological questions.

But, in either case, in your first-year metaphysics course, you shouldn't be surprised if epistemological questions arise. A famous example of this link is in Descartes, who tries to solve metaphysical questions (what exists?) with epistemological methods (what can I doubt/not doubt exists?). Another example would be Plato, for whom the 'forms' or 'ideas' are an answer to two questions at once: 'What is X?' and 'How do we know X?'

There is also an important link between metaphysics and the philosophy of religion. To take the most obvious example, all of the main arguments for the existence of a God have metaphysical roots. The notions of perfection and existence in the ontological proof, for example. Or again, the notion of causation and first cause (or cause of the whole) in the cosmological proof. It is very likely that such arguments and considerations will have a place on a first-year metaphysics course.

There is yet another important link between metaphysics and ethics, which most frequently has something to do with the concept of freedom. It is often argued that my action can only be characterised as 'ethical' or 'unethical' if I am free to act otherwise than I do. But whether I am free in this sense might be a matter for metaphysics to decide. First of all, because it concerns a question about the type of existing thing that I am. And second, because it is a question that could not possibly be addressed by any science – indeed, it would appear that in order to get going, any science has to assume that its object is not 'free', but rather behaves according to describable laws that are outside the object's control. It is possible that such questions will appear on first-year metaphysics courses, but it is equally likely to appear in ethical theory courses instead.

The above paragraph reveals also another key sub-topic in metaphysics: the philosophy of mind. What, for example, is consciousness? Is it simply identical with what goes on in my brain, and if so, how could we prove it, and would it be possible ever to 'translate' between brain process and thoughts? Another frequently encountered problem is the nature of personal identity – what makes me, me? If, for example, my mind were miraculously transported into another person's body, would I still be the same person I was? Although the first of these problems is clearly related to the science of neuro-physiology, and the second (perhaps less clearly) to psychology, neither of these sciences could answer these philosophical questions. Rather, they are well-defined sciences precisely because they *assume* an answer (or a range

Plato (c. 428–c. 348 BC) Plato is one of the greatest of philosophers, and (although there were many philosophers before him) essentially the founder of the Western philosophical approach. This he called 'dialectic', which includes the careful definition and analysis of key ideas, and the construction of arguments along valid logical lines. (However, it was Aristotle, after him, who would first codify what these 'valid logical lines' actually were.) Plato is known through around twenty-five dialogues. These take the form of dramas, with normally three or more speaking parts. In most of the dialogues, the main speaking part is Socrates. Socrates was an important historical figure, and Plato's teacher, but for the most part what the character Socrates says has more to do with Plato than with the historical Socrates. (To what extent, in any given dialogue, the figure of Socrates can be considered a mouthpiece for what Plato really thought is a matter of debate.) Plato is important for a number of philosophical ideas, among them the theory of forms. Plato argued that unless we posited the existence of, and our mind's familiarity with, a set of 'forms' or 'ideas', then it would be impossible to understand how we could know anything. These forms, because they would have to be known equally by all minds, and must also be unchanging, could not be real things. Plato accordingly suggested, with various inflections, that the forms must be a different, and more real, form of existence. However, 'what' the forms are is a secondary consideration for the most part, although it tends to obsess modern readers. Notice how epistemological and metaphysical considerations are here closely linked. However, it is important to realise that these epistemological and metaphysical ideas frequently appear in the contexts of dialogues the chief concern of which is goodness, virtue, or other aspects of excellence of character. Thus for Plato, ethical considerations are paramount, and metaphysical speculation only a tool to serve that end.

of possible answers) to the questions. In other words, because neuro-physiology assumes that everything within its remit is a matter of brain activity or structure, it could not investigate the question of whether that assumption is valid. So, again, we are back to how we defined philosophy at the beginning of the book. Philosophy of mind is an important area in philosophy, not least because it is an area where philosophy can be successfully interdisciplinary – for example, interacting with artificial-intelligence research.

Finally, let us clear up a couple of misunderstandings. (1) These days 'metaphysics' is often used to describe the writings or teachings of 'new age' thinkers. Now, while it may be the case that such thinkers are, in fact, metaphysicians in the above sense, this is quite accidental. For outside of philosophy the word simply describes the 'mystical' or 'spiritual' dimension of their thought. Before you buy a book about 'metaphysics', make sure it is *philosophical* metaphysics! (2) Similarly, 'metaphysics' is used to describe anything that is difficult to understand, or very abstract, and is often used with the pejorative connotation that it is *deliberately* difficult to understand and has something to hide. In other words, 'hot air'. While there is no question that a great deal of philosophical metaphysics is difficult (and thus *appears* to be hot air) that is often because of the fundamental level at which it challenges our deeply ingrained assumptions about things.

A sample mind-map of an essay on Descartes' account of space is given in the section on essay writing in Part Two.

2.2.2 Epistemology and philosophy of science

Insofar as philosophers have always sought *truth* and tried to avoid *illusions* or *mere opinion*, epistemology has been an important concern. Epistemology means the philosophical enquiry into the origin and nature of knowledge. Although frequently linked, these are two distinct enquiries. We can ask what knowledge is (for example, is knowledge a justified and true representation of the world?), without necessarily asking how that knowledge comes about (does it derive from innate ideas, for example, or from direct sensory acquaintance with the world?).

Berkeley, George (1685–1753) Irish philosopher who, in response to the work of Descartes and Locke, produced an idealist philosophy. Berkeley felt that Locke's empiricism, while perfectly correct in its identification of the importance of simple ideas of sense, led to dangerous scepticism because Locke also held a broadly realist position. That is, 'behind' or 'outside' those simple ideas lay a material world. But because all our minds have ideas of sense, there is a gap between mind and world such that the world could never be fully understood or even proved to exist (this scepticism, of course, was Descartes' problem in his method of doubt). Berkeley removed such scepticism by simply denying even the possibility of such matter, and claiming that only ideas and minds exist. Saying 'I see an apple' and 'I have the simple sense idea of an apple' are completely equivalent statements – that is, 'to exist' and 'to be perceived' are the same. My ideas exhibit constancy and regularity not because of some world of material substances, but because all ideas also exist in, and are regulated by, the mind of God. Although few philosophers subsequently accepted Berkeley's conclusions, his arguments against the epistemological and metaphysical assumptions of Descartes and Locke have fared much better.

Traditionally, epistemology showed up in the work of philosophers in two main ways. First, as a secondary issue that sought to legitimate some primary philosophical enterprise. For example, arguably, Plato wasn't terribly interested in knowledge *per se*; instead, he was interested in goodness or virtue. However, in order to make claims about such matters, he had to address the secondary question of 'How does one *know* anything about the Good?' But, second, some philosophers considered understanding knowledge as the primary task for philosophy, and actually acquiring knowledge about particular issues to be the secondary task. Kant might be considered a good example here: his transcendental philosophy tried to establish what the conditions of knowledge were (for example, the conditions of a scientific knowledge of natural phenomena) but the task of actually acquiring that knowledge was a scientific, not a philosophical, one. Both the epistemologies of Plato and Kant are likely to receive some attention on first-year epistemology courses.

Key epistemological notions that are very likely to show up on first-year courses are *innate ideas*, and *empiricism*. Innate ideas are representations of how the world is that the mind finds itself equipped with, as if 'from birth'. Some interpretations of Plato's theory of forms would have it that Plato believed in innate ideas, and Descartes certainly did. In brief, innate ideas are an attempt to solve the problem of how we could have knowledge that was universal or necessary (the usual examples are metaphysical statements like 'nothing can come from nothing', or the axioms of geometry). No experience of a thing, or any series of experiences of a thing, could show our knowledge of it to be universal or necessary. Empiricism is normally represented as the direct opposite of innate ideas theory (Locke certainly thought so, since he devoted the whole first book of his *Essay Concerning Human Understanding* to an attack on innate ideas). Empiricists generally claim that all knowledge (and, for that matter, all false beliefs too) are ultimately derived from our sensory acquaintance with the world, and from nowhere else. Taken to one extreme, as in Hume, this amounts to the claim that *no* knowledge about the world could be guaranteed universal or necessary.

The debate between philosophers of innate ideas and empiricists concerns itself with the *origin* of knowledge. A key problem in the question of the *nature* of knowledge is a debate concerning what it means to say that something is true. A peculiar, but highly influential, theory of truth was advanced by William James (together with his fellow pragmatists), towards the end of the nineteenth century. This is the subject of a sample examination answer below. The sample presentation that follows concerns 'abstract ideas': an attempt to understand how one idea or word might come to stand for more than one thing. Locke and Berkeley are key figures in this debate, and the presentation ends with two brief arguments that have a Wittgensteinian flavour about them.

Wittgenstein, Ludwig (1889–1951) Austrian philosopher who spent much of his career at Cambridge University.

Wittgenstein's philosophy is usually divided into early and later stages. The early work, and above all his *Tractatus Logic-Philosophicus* (1921), is an attempt to understand the way that language reaches the world by way of a 'picture-theory' of meaning. A sentence represents a state-of-affairs in the world by modelling it: the structure of the sentence is related to the structure of the state-of-affairs, and the elements of the sentence are related to elements within the state-of-affairs. All true sentences can be derived logically from 'atomic' or basic propositions that represent basic facts, and the 'world' is the sum of all such facts. The second stage of Wittgenstein's work begins in 1929 and, in the opinion of most, culminates in the *Philosophical Investigations* (published posthumously in 1953). The ideal abstraction of language and thought from the world they represent has disappeared, and Wittgenstein is now interested in how language gets used, how it plays a role in people's lives. He describes these various roles as 'language games'. The important points here are: that there is always more than one language game, that no meta-language (a language that tries to describe language) could ever fully capture the language game, and thus that philosophy gets into trouble when it tries to reduce all language games down to one (such as logic, or science). The necessarily social dimension of language has implications for first-person conceptions of mind and meaning (especially but not exclusively Descartes). Wittgenstein remains one of the most influential, and endlessly discussed, philosophers of the past century.

Sample examination answer

Question: Discuss one or two of James' arguments for a pragmatist conception of truth? (1 hour)

Writing at the end of the nineteenth century, James observed the extraordinary success of the sciences in achieving things, but at the same time a rapid increase in the number of different scientific theories being proposed. As we will see, the only way both of these things could be the case is if our understanding of what it means to propose a theory in science, and what the truth of that theory means, is misguided. James aims to replace the prevalent theory of truth with a pragmatist one.

[*A concise introduction that seems, at least, to tell us what the examination answer is going to do. But, it neither tells us what a pragmatist theory of truth is, nor does it fully inform us how the student intends to establish it. So, an acceptable introduction, but it could have been improved by another sentence or two that sketches the content that is to follow.*]

The success of the sciences included not just physics, which seemed to have been gathering steam since Newton, but relatively newer sciences as well: modern medicine, psychology, economics, and so forth. It would seem logical that as new truths were uncovered, there would be fewer things for scientists to disagree about. That is, fewer things that were as yet poorly understood and thus lead to a variety of possible theories being put forward. Dunn claims that Kant formulated a 'regulative' idea of the unity of science a century before James. According to Kant, the sciences should be advancing towards a *single* and *uniquely true* theoretical description of each of their objects. Since the objects were all part of nature in general, the all the sciences together should be converging towards a single theoretical account of nature. But, as James saw it, in each of these sciences, each new advance did not reduce the amount of debate between specialists. On the contrary, at the time he was writing, James noted that even in very advanced sciences, the number of competing theoretical models being advanced was not decreasing but instead *increasing*. Just like in pre-scientific days, or in the early years of a science, there were many theories. But, unlike those early days, these theories are not simply unsupported by evidence and experiment. Rather, they all *work*: they make predictions tested by observation, they all solve problems, they all fit in with some other popular theories. How could this be?

[A good paragraph, with the points made clearly and crisply. Note the reference to the fictional Dunn and the non-fictional Kant. It all leads up to an intriguing question that the student feels confident she can answer.]

So why, James asks, given all this, do we not call all of these competing theories 'true'? It is because of a metaphysical model of truth that dates back at least to Plato. It is usually called the 'correspondence' theory of truth. A proposition is true if and only if it corresponds exactly with reality. In Plato, for example, reality meant the forms. A truth was true because it corresponded with the forms. Knowing the truth means having something like a 'copy' of reality in one's mind. This so-called 'correspondence' theory of truth certainly seemed to have common sense on its side. But it is precisely what James sees as the problem.

[No doubt a Plato scholar would have a few things to say about the caricature of Plato's theory of forms. Normally, such a quick and cavalier distortion of a philosopher's life work would be strongly discouraged. But this answer is not interested in understanding Plato, but in providing a quick sketch of an idea that helps us to understand, by way of contrast, another idea. So, she can get away with it. However, there are too many 'it's in that paragraph – that is, too many pronouns and it is not always easy for the reader to figure out what the pronoun refers to.]

Suppose there were five competing theories within science X. All of the five make different claims about the ultimate nature of the objects of X. But, in terms of predicting how those objects will behave, all five have similar levels of success. Surely, it would be a marvellous coincidence if of five theories that work, only one should be true and the others entirely false? Much better to suppose, with James, that this correspondence between a theory and some real world is just nonsense. James redefines the key concepts in this way: the meaning of a statement is equivalent to the actions we would perform if we believed it, and the truth of a statement is equivalent to those actions 'working' or having good effects.

[The 'marvellous coincidence' argument is a bit weak. What's wrong with 'marvellous coincidences' every once in a while? The student should have spent a bit more time on this section, especially given the length of time she spent setting up the problem in the previous few paragraphs. A lesson worth learning: whatever else you have to rush, don't rush the pivotal move in an argument! Notice also that the definition of 'meaning' and 'truth' in pragmatism was probably memorised, and wheeled out at the appropriate moment. This is a good idea for examinations: memorise a couple of key definitions, especially where precision would be helpful. Obviously, though, only use them if they are appropriate to the answer!]

Another argument James uses is to ask how is the term 'true' actually used in our everyday life? When I say something is true, I may *think* that I mean, abstractly, that it is a copy of some reality. But what is the evidence that that is what I mean by 'truth'? It is much more likely that by 'true' I mean the relation that the statement has to other ideas or actions. For example, if I say 'It is raining outside', you don't immediately start asking whether or not my statement corresponds to some reality. Rather, you start moaning about getting wet, or wishing that you had brought an umbrella, or glad because now it might not be so hot outside, or wish that the weather people on the news would get their act together. In other words, first of all, the *meaning* of the statement cannot be distinguished from the practical implications of the statement. And the *truth* of the statement consists in going outside, into the rain, and actually moaning about getting wet, or actually wishing that you had brought an umbrella, and so on. Truth as abstract, ideal correspondence with reality-in-itself is just not something we worry about very often, if at all. Indeed, if we did stop to think about correspondence, would it help us? How do you *know* my statement is true? By planning and performing a practical test: you go outside and see if you get wet. Correspondence could be established in no other way than through this practical test, so why then do we think that truth means something *different* from the practical test? Truth is established by successful outcomes.

[*The second argument in this essay is discussed in greater detail, and with a nice example. The implications of the argument are forcefully and clearly stated. One problem with this paragraph, though, is that there are* two *arguments here: the second one being that 'correspondence' can meaning nothing other than successful, practical outcomes. The two should have been more clearly differentiated.*]

Pragmatism is therefore an account of how our minds deal with everyday reality. In our everyday lives, truths mean successful practical outcomes. But in the first argument concerning scientific theories, James also says that this is true even for the most abstract theoretical concerns. There, too, the meaning of truth ultimately boils down to what difference it would make that something is true.

[*A good examination answer conclusion: very brief restatement of what has been argued for, and how.*]

Sample presentation outline for the question 'Are there abstract ideas? Why or why not?'

What follows is a sample group presentation. First, a set of over-head projector slides the group used. Then, a sketch of their text. The assumption is of a group presentation (three individuals), and a speaking time of approximately twenty minutes. How long is twenty minutes? From 2,500 up to 3,000 words of text should do nicely. Please see Part Two of this book for practical advice about presentations.

Are there abstract ideas?
Why or Why Not?

Presentation by Kirsty Brown, David Jones and Roger Smith

● Section one: what epistemological problems are abstract
ideas supposed to solve?

● Section two: versions of the
concept of abstract ideas.

● Section three: objections

Section One: What epistemological problems are abstract ideas supposed to solve?

● Imagine every object has a proper name.

● Would thought/communication be possible?

– Problem of anticipating the future (Carrey 1998: 109).

– Learning names.

[This is the title slide, including the overall title of the presentation, the presenters, and the headings of each section. Section one, by the way, will serve as an introduction: in effect, it is setting up the whole discussion by asking: 'Why are we interested in abstract ideas at all?'. The title slide should be put back on the screen between each section (so your audience knows where they are in the overall plan) and perhaps also at the end (to help remind your audience of what they have heard).]

[This slide is for the first section. It gives the title of the section, then two sub-topics. Under the second sub-topic are two further topics. In this way, a fairly complex structure is made clear to the audience.

Notice that the format of each slide is the same. This looks professional, and makes it easy for the audience to understand. This is why it's a good idea for creating the slides to be the responsibility of just one person in the group!]

Section Two: versions of the concept of abstract ideas.

- Natural kinds – e.g. the naming of animals in Genesis.

- Nominalism – grouping things together under one property.

- Locke and abstract ideas – we can form an idea that refers to all instances of a particular type.

Quotation from Locke

'The use of words then being to stand as outward marks of our internal ideas, and those ideas being taken from particular things, if every particular idea that we take in should have a distinct name, names must be endless. To prevent this, the mind makes the particular ideas received from particular objects to become general; which is done by considering them as they are in the mind . . . separate from all other existences and the circumstances of real existence, as time, place, or any other concomitant ideas. This is called abstraction, whereby ideas taken from particular beings become general representatives of all of the same kind.' (Locke 1990: 74)

[As a slide, fine. But one wonders why, if the focus of the presentation is going to be on Locke and his critics, the other two 'versions' need to be discussed at all? Just because you know something is no excuse for putting it in. Keep it relevant!]

[This slide is not a new section, but a lengthy but important quotation concerning the third sub-topic on the previous slide.]

Section Three: objections to concept of abstract ideas.

1. Two Interpretations of Locke. (Angoulis 1980: 39)

– Berkeley's criticism: there are only particular ideas.

– Berkeley's proposal: customary connections between particulars.

Objections, cont.

2. Suppose we have a particular idea of white, and from it abstract a general idea of whiteness. We put this idea away in our mental 'filing cabinet'. Then, along comes another particular idea. Is it white? We compare it to our remembered idea of whiteness. But there is no way of knowing (no external corroboration) that our memory is correct. Saying that

something is white means more than just saying 'it looks like what I remember white looking like'. The notion that abstraction is a personal mental process cannot be correct.

Similarly, Locke assumes a gap between the abstract idea and the real things it refers to. The abstract idea, and my employment of it, is a personal matter, and the idea is a different thing from any real object and any employment. But, if that is true, then there could be no way for someone else to judge whether we had used the idea correctly, and thus no way for us to communicate about the idea of white itself (Casillas 1992: 121). But for Locke, the whole reason for positing abstract ideas was that they permit communication.

Locke's account must be insufficient, and Berkeley's alternative is also. The whole attempt to talk about abstract ideas, or mental 'customary connections', is misguided.

[Section three has also been split into two slides. In this case, each slide is a summary of one argument. Although this slide is brief, because the group is swapping to a different presenter for the second half of this section, it's best to use a new slide.]

[These two, related arguments are, roughly, a Wittgensteinian approach to the issue. The philosophical ideas may be interesting, but this is a lousy slide.

The problem with this slide is that there is too much information on it. The aim is for your slides to be a navigation aid to your audience, not a chunk of text. Otherwise, the audience spends so much time reading and puzzling over your slide, they stop listening to the presentation! Where ever possible, just put headings on to your slides, not summaries.]

[N.B.The group might wish to have a slide for the concluding remarks, rather than just putting the title slide back up. This would be necessary, for example, if (1) the group plans on saying something in the conclusion other than review what has gone before – e.g. a very carefully worded answer to the title question; or (2) if the group is suggesting questions for their audience.]

Script

Brown: Good morning. My name is Kirsty Brown. Today, my colleagues and I are giving a presentation on the problem of abstract ideas. We will begin by discussing what are the philosophical problems that lead to the proposal of abstract ideas. David Jones here will be discussing these in our first section. Then, we will look at three different proposals that try to solve these problems. In our second section, Roger Smith to my left will be discussing these proposals. Most of our effort will be put into understanding John Locke's famous version. In the third section, David will be talking about Berkeley's objection to Locke's version, and how Berkeley thought he could solve the problems from our first section without having to talk about abstraction at all. Then, I will look at a couple of arguments inspired by Wittgenstein. These arguments claim that both Locke and Berkeley provide insufficient accounts, and are perhaps approaching the question in entirely the wrong way. Finally, Roger will sum up our arguments, and open the floor for questions.

[The introduction is just like that for an essay, except that you need to identify who you are. In a presentation given by a group, there is much potential for confusing the audience by swapping presenters too quickly, or by their roles within the presentation not being clear.]

Jones: Thank you, Kirsty. Imagine that every object has a proper name, and there are no general nouns. Instead of being able to say or think 'table', I would have to refer to this table by a unique name that had nothing in common with any other table. Then, there would have to be an infinite number of names . . . *[The rest of Jones's section deleted.]*

Smith: Thank you, David. In this section, I will discuss three philosophical proposals that seek to overcome the bizarre situation that David described. The first of these we'll call 'natural kinds theory'. The classic example of this is Adam's naming of the animals in Genesis. For each essential type of animal, there is one name . . .

The second of these proposals is nominalism . . .

The third of the proposals is the one we shall look at in most detail, because it has been so influential. According to Locke, we can form 'abstract ideas'. That is, we can form an idea that refers to all instances of a particular type, by taking away all the other properties that happen to attach to the instances. Let us look at the passage where Locke introduces this idea . . .

[Notice that Smith has begun his bit by reminding the audience of where we are in the structure of the presentation overall. Notice also that he clearly marks the beginning of each sub-section.]

Jones: We are now moving on to section three of our presentation, which looks at objections to these (and especially Locke's) proposals. I'll discuss the first major objection, that of Berkeley. Kirsty will discuss the second objection. The first thing we need to point out is that there are two interpretations of Locke: is the abstract idea a particular idea (an 'exemplar') that signifies generally, or a genuinely general idea that is not at all an idea of a particular? The latter is the more usual interpretation, so we'll assume it here. Berkeley, however, felt that this was absurd . . .

Brown: The second objection is to the whole idea of seeking a solution to the problem in internal mental contents or actions. Suppose we have a particular idea of white . . .

[This is the section that has the lousy slide. If Brown is just going to read off the slide, wouldn't it be better just to shut up and let the audience read for themselves?]

Smith: In this presentation we have looked at . . .
Are there any questions?

[Hmm, how likely is it that anyone is going to speak up at this point? You need to encourage your audience to ask questions. A good idea is to put some suggested questions into your conclusion. For example, Smith could say 'Our group was wondering whether Berkeley is begging the question. Doesn't he just assume that there are only particular ideas, and on that basis, not surprisingly, shows there cannot be general ideas?' The group might also wish to propose that their audience mulls over a new example or hypothetical scenario that seems particularly interesting or troubling. Having some questions out there at the end should encourage others to arise. And, believe it or not, you want questions!]

2.2.3 Ethics, applied ethics and political philosophy

Although they tend to be closely related, there are really three areas of philosophy here. Ethics is the broad study of the origin, validity and meaning of our ideas about goodness, and of how these ideas could result in good acts. 'Goodness' and 'good' are to be understood in a moral sense. That is, what is 'good' is what 'ought' to be the case, rather than what simply 'is' the case. Clearly, this is an instance of philosophy doing its proper job as we defined it above. For, we are asking, 'What are the foundations of any claim that "x is good"?'. And asking this question is different from being a good person, or doing good deeds – it is a philosophical question. This might be seen as a weakness: students are often surprised (and a little disappointed) that courses on ethics do not tell them *what* the good is and thus *how* they should behave. Instead, ethics courses either consider various general accounts of how the good should be determined (utilitarianism, for example), or evaluate varying solutions to what it would mean to say an act was good. (This latter approach is frequently called 'metaethics'; the prefix 'meta-' means the same here as for 'metaphysics'). In other words, that here is an investigation of the meaning of the basic concepts of ethics, which may be considered a fundamental investigation with respect to the question 'How should I act?')

Above, we distinguished between what *is* the case and what *ought* to be the case. You should be aware that the nature of this ought/is distinction (drawn very clearly by Hume), and its validity, is a key topic in ethics and is very likely to show up in your first-year course. Other questions in ethics could border on the metaphysical (such as 'Are human actions ever *free*?'), or could employ epistemology (such as 'When I say that "X is good" what type of knowledge, if any, is that, and how do I know it?'), but most often concern the nature and meaning of ideas of the good ('What does it mean to say that "X is good"? Does it, for example, mean something like "X will lead to increased happiness" as the utilitarians argued?').

Utilitarianism An important theory of ethics that originated in Britain in the late eighteenth and early nineteenth centuries and had a significant role in the liberalisation of Western social policy over the past two centuries. Bentham and Mill are the key figures. Utilitarians believe that, in general, a good act is defined as that act that leads to the greatest increase in happiness for all concerned (or the greatest decrease in unhappiness). In other words, acts are judged by their consequences, and the consequences are judged with respect to the overall quantity of happiness. Utilitarians differ on precisely how 'happiness' is to be defined and determined, on whether or not individual agents should be given responsibility for predicting the consequences of each of their actions, and on whose happiness counts and whether all count equally. Increasingly subtle, and sometimes radical, versions of utilitarianism are still employed by philosophers today, especially when discussing issues in applied ethics.

Applied ethics concerns what should be considered good in specific types of cases. For example, whether the act of euthanasia is ever good, and if so under what circumstances, or, again, whether vegetarianism is a moral act. In other words, while ethics tends to look at broad issues concerning the good (what it means, how it is justified), applied ethics tries to work out how general laws of the good function when we are confronted with specific situations. There are many areas of applied ethics: the examples above fall under 'medical ethics' and what is often broadly called 'environmental ethics', but you may also encounter 'business ethics' and others specific to certain professions. It might appear that applied ethics is always dependent upon ethics in the broader sense: one must know what basic principles of action are good before one could apply them to specific cases. But many applied ethicists argue that such an approach is hopelessly abstract and could never yield results; thus, they claim, it is better to work through issues situation by situation.

Political philosophy concerns the nature and validity of political organisation of all kinds. It borders on ethical philosophy insofar as one typical question of political philosophy (and, indeed, historically speaking, the original question) is 'What is the best form of political organisation?' This notion of 'best' is at least analogous to the moral 'good', since it asks what ought to be the case rather than merely what is the case. As in ethics, there are often two stages to this question: first, deciding what 'best' means, politically, which usually comes down to the question 'What should be the purpose of political organisation?' For example, Aristotle argues that the purpose of the state is to enable human beings to attain most completely the life proper to human beings (which he also describes). Second, what actual form of political organisation most closely realises this 'purpose'? Aristotle, armed with his treatment of the 'life proper to humans', analysed many real and imagined forms of political organisation for their effectiveness in reaching this end.

This second half of the 'best' question, however, is itself a key problem for political philosophy, which is often studied on its own. This involves understanding the fundamental elements of political organisations: what, for example, is the nature of co-operation, right, competition, or power? Notice, once again, how neatly this falls into our definition of philosophy. Political science tends to concern itself with how a given political system functions; to do so, it needs to assume an answer to a question such as 'What is the nature of power?' in order to begin studying a given instance of power. Asking that fundamental question is the task of the political philosopher.

There are still other questions frequently encountered in first-year political philosophy courses. For example, is it ever right to disobey the laws of the state, perhaps in an act of civil disobedience, or even in an act of revolution?

Aristotle (384–322 BC) Aristotle was Plato's pupil but, in his mature years, disagreed with his teacher about many fundamental points. One new idea of Aristotle's that is of enormous importance for his writings on politics, ethics, aesthetics and even metaphysics, is teleology. Aristotle argued that all phenomena could be understood most fundamentally from the point of view of their 'telos', which means end or purpose. So, the chief questions of political philosophy are not 'What is power?' or 'What is justice?' or some question of that type, but rather 'What is political organisation for, what is it supposed to achieve?' The answer, Aristotle claims, is that political organisation aims to realise the 'good life' for human beings, which involves virtue and a level of material wealth sufficient to allow virtue. He asks a similar question in, for example, his analysis of tragic drama. The question 'What is tragedy?' is dominated by the question 'what is tragedy for, what are dramatists trying to do when they write tragedies?' The answer in this case involves the somewhat mysterious notion of catharsis, a purging or cleansing of the emotions. Such questions and answers are typical of Aristotle's philosophical method. Of all Aristotle's writings, you are most likely to come across the work on ethics on a first-year course.

2.2.4 Aesthetics

For much of the history of philosophy, aesthetics has been predominantly the philosophical study of the phenomena of beauty, sublime, or other such. These phenomena are considered the key features of fine art. They are what make fine art 'fine'. In addition, these phenomena are the key features of certain extraordinary and valuable *natural* objects (the beauty of a rainbow, the sublimity of a canyon). So, aesthetics fits in nicely with our definition of philosophy above: we are asking about the fundamental features of beautiful art, say, or sublime nature, about what makes them beautiful or sublime. It would be difficult, and perhaps impossible, for such questions to be asked by an artist, without her ceasing to be an artist. (Although, of course, there are many very interesting works of art that seem to function precisely by raising such questions.) In fact, the use of the term 'aesthetics' for this area of philosophy originates late in the eighteenth century. However, the discussion of these or related ideas does date back to the Greek period. For example, Plato concerned himself with the question of whether an art object, however apparently beautiful, could ever be 'true' – and indeed, whether the pretension of art to 'truth' was in fact philosophically dangerous. Aristotle tackled the subject of tragedy, asking what the purpose of tragedy was in distinction from other forms of writing. Questions of the 'truth' of art, and of the purpose of art, remain highly significant in aesthetics today.

Since the eighteenth century, a chief question of aesthetics was (and for many philosophers still is) 'What differentiates beautiful or sublime *objects* from ordinary objects?' Note that this is different from the question 'What differentiates the *experience* of beauty or sublimity from ordinary experiences?', another chief question. Not surprisingly, an important philosophical debate arises around which of these questions is the best one to be asking. If you ask the first question, you seem to be claiming that beauty is a property of the object itself, and thus a beautiful painting would have to be beautiful even if no one ever looked at it. If you ask the second question, you seem to be claiming that beauty is a property of an experience of an object, and the 'beautiful' painting is not beautiful until viewed, and even then it is not the painting *per se* that is beautiful. Another question in contemporary aesthetics that you might well encounter can be expressed in this way: 'To what extent is our taste for beauty or the sublime socially constructed, rather than natural, and indeed constructed precisely in order to serve certain political or economic interests?' A closely related, but simpler, version of this question is: 'Are the typical aesthetic questions about beauty or sublime misleading with respect to the real nature of art?'

Aesthetics is often divided into sub-categories by the genre of the object under discussion. For example, you might come across 'literary aesthetics', 'film aesthetics', and so on.

2.2.5 The philosophy of religion

Without question, you will come across the classic arguments for the existence of God on your first-year philosophy of religion course. There are four such classic types of arguments: the *ontological*, the *cosmological*, the argument from *design*, and the *moral* argument. There are also a number of variations. Each of these is indeed a classic, the kind of philosophical argument that seems to generate interesting ideas and debates inexhaustibly. What is important to remember is that none of these arguments are, strictly speaking, dead – new and extraordinarily subtle versions keep being proposed by philosophers even today, along with new and equally subtle objections. You should also keep in mind that, with all these different versions around, no one statement of an argument (or of an objection to it) is definitive. In short, on such courses you should be wary of simply repeating the stock forms and stock objections – much more fun to dig a bit deeper. Also note that these classic arguments are good examples of how we defined philosophy above. Each of the arguments is trying to investigate down to the fundamental nature of the world and its inhabitants. This investigation is not one that could be carried out by the ordinary 'sciences' of the world, whether that is physics or ethics.

Other important topics that you may well come across on your philosophy of religion course are: What is the nature of religious faith, and can it ever be justified or, proved wrong? What is the nature of religious language and, although it sometimes appears to be an employment of language in a perfectly ordinary sense, does it in fact function in the same way as ordinary language? A related question is this one: given that our language and concepts function for the description of worldly things, in what sense is it possible to describe the features of God? (This question is clearly related to the classic arguments for the existence of God, all of which function in part by *describing* God: as 'perfect', 'infinite', 'first cause', 'designer', or whatever.) The problem of evil is also likely to crop up (why would a perfect God have created a universe in which there is suffering?) as may issues concerning the possibility and nature of an afterlife (for example, what implications does it have for our conception of what it means to be a person?). These latter questions can all be seen as versions of the religious language problem.

It should also be pointed out that philosophy of religion courses are by no means just for the religious. Much of the greatest philosophy falls under this heading, if for no other reason than for many centuries it was considered to be of the highest importance. Moreover, the implications of all the above topics are huge, and the ideas upon which they are based important, such that the significance of the philosophy of religion extends well beyond religion, strictly speaking. For example, the issue above on the nature of religious language takes us straight to the heart of the philosophical question of the nature of language in general.

Sample examination answer

Question: How should we understand Kant's 'moral argument' for the existence of God? (1 hour)

[A slightly unusual question. Clearly it is asking for an exposition of the argument, and probably also for some critical analysis of it. However, it may be looking for some contextualisation too, if we are going to 'understand' the argument well. How to approach such a question will be guided by what happened in class. Try to adopt the same way of tackling problems as your tutor did.]

Kant's 'moral argument' attempts to prove the existence of a God, and thus joins the three other classic proofs (ontological, cosmological and design). But there is an important difference: Kant claims that the moral argument is entirely practical, whereas the others are theoretical (which is precisely why, in Kant's opinion, the other three do not work). In the following I will first discuss this distinction between practical and theoretical, and I will then turn to the argument itself.

[Perhaps the style is a bit cumbersome, but otherwise a nice introduction. Locates the argument in a very broad context, introduces the key distinction, and then gives a brief essay map.]

A theoretical way of thinking, Kant says, takes the form of knowledge. That is, it aims at an essentially passive representation of how the world is. In its aim to acquire knowledge, the theoretical is limited to the representation of things in the experienceable world. Since any argument for the existence of God must try to represent the existence of something that is *outside* the experienceable world, such arguments must fail. The practical, however, concerns the will and the acts of will, and especially moral acts. That is, essentially active attempts to bring about what ought to be. These two distinctions characterise the theoretical and the practical: activity and passivity; Hume's 'is' and 'ought'. Kant claims that his moral argument only functions within the practical, and thus, even if the argument is successful, it does not produce *knowledge* of God's existence.

[This paragraph fulfils the first half of the plan. Notice also that it fills in some of the details from the introduction – why the theoretical arguments must fail, for example. In so doing, it not only explains the distinction theoretical/practical, but also explains why that distinction is important.]

In Kant's moral philosophy, an act can be considered moral only if we act out of duty (that is, act simply on the basis of moral laws) and do not take into consideration what the consequences of our actions might be. If, Kant argues, it is morally wrong to lie, then it is wrong regardless of the circumstances and what may happen as a consequence of lying. This purity of the moral law is precisely what guarantees its morality. For, Kant says, if we allowed the consequences of our actions to influence our behaviour, then we would be allowing non-moral issues to influence our morality, and that would destroy morality, he thinks. (The reason for this has to do with the nature of moral freedom, but we cannot go into that here.) Nevertheless, the moral action has to be possible, otherwise willing it makes no sense. A moral law that demanded all pigs should fly would be absurd (Brookes' example). Relatedly, Dover argues that if following our duty *always* seemed to lead to bad moral consequences (if every time we gave to charity, ten extra people died), then it would be impossible to believe that acting morally was ever really possible. The core of Kant's moral argument lies in this issue of the mere possibility of our moral acts. One might at this point object that Kant is allowing consequences to influence duty in through the back door. However, there seem to be two different concepts of 'possibility' here.

[Notice the use of a couple very quick examples in order to illustrate the abstract points being made; the first example is Kant's own, the second is briefly referenced to a fictional author named 'Brookes'. Another fictional author 'Dover' is cited as the source of a briefly expressed argument.]

[Notice also the disclaimer about 'moral freedom'. The implication is not that the student hasn't got enough time, but rather that further analysis of this issue is unimportant to the argument. You can't talk about everything, obviously. But do make sure that when you leave something out, (1) you draw attention to it (you might get credit for your broader knowledge), and (2) that it really is unimportant for answering the question.]

Our free will acting in accordance with duty makes moral action possible in general, Kant claims. Nothing affects the possibility of duty itself. But what makes real moral action possible in the real world? The will must assume that acting according to duty will tend to be physically possible, and that duty will at least normally bring about good consequences. Otherwise, the idea of obeying duty would just seem absurd. It is as if, in its moral action, the will posits the truth of the following proposition: 'The world is such that it tends to "co-operate" with my moral action.' (Speaking of 'truths' and 'propositions' is of course the language of theoretical philosophy.) So what guarantees this truth?

[This paragraph tries to detail, first, what the 'two different concepts of possibility' are, and, second, what are the implications of this whole question of the possibility of moral acts. The fact that this paragraph was doing two jobs could have been made clearer. Also, the significance of the parenthetical comment towards the end could do with more explanation – many readers might be tempted to say, 'so what?'.]

Kant argues that no theoretical (that is, scientific) analysis of the world could establish this truth, since no scientific analysis is competent to ask what duty is, or what 'good' consequences are. In other words, nature understood scientifically, does not obviously 'tend' towards co-operation in my moral enterprise. This, however, is far from clear, since many have tried to use evolution theory, or economic theory, to show that 'natural' processes yield results that look an awful lot like that which people consider good. (Another objection would be the unjustified introduction of an anthropomorphism in the notion of 'co-operation'.) Kant has to suppose that *any* such 'scientific' approach to the fulfilment of morality must fail. If we suppose this, then it would follow that the guarantee of the will's assumption cannot be 'in' the world. It must be something *outside* the world (and thus outside the province of theoretical thinking). Moreover, this something outside the world must have absolute power over the world, and be a moral intelligence also. In other words, God.

[The student is hurrying. Neither of the two objections, and especially the second, is properly developed.]

It is important to remember that all this is within the context of the acting will's 'assumptions'. The existence of a God therefore is posited by and for my moral action. It is not a theoretical piece of knowledge – instead, it is a moral faith.

[The student seems to have ended things in a rush. This is not uncommon in examination answers, of course. Still, though, it would be nice to see a few more sentences explaining the last sentence and referring the reader back to the various objections made against Kant's argument, and perhaps also how devastating to the argument the objections really are. Still, this is a good answer which makes attempts to lay out things in a logical fashion, and to evaluate definitions and arguments.]

2.2.6 Ancient philosophy

Unfortunately, coverage of ancient philosophy often consists solely of Plato and/or Aristotle. To be sure, these two are among the greatest and most enduringly interesting of philosophers. These two set the agenda of both the problems, and the methods, of 'Western' philosophy ever since. Nevertheless, it's a bit like saying that the only two cities in Europe are London and Paris.

So, from other sections we know something about Plato and Aristotle. Who are some of the others? Before Plato, and before Socrates, there are the long sequence of philosophers known as the 'Pre-Socratics' for obvious reasons. Heraclitus, Parmenides, Democritus and Zeno of Elea are four you might well come across. But after Aristotle, the so-called ancient world continued for centuries. We have Zeno of Citium, the Greek founder of stoicism, which was extremely important during the Roman period, including the emperor Marcus Aurelius as one of its chief exponents; Epicurus, the founder of Epicurianism (not surprisingly), which was heavily influenced by Democritus and taken up in the Roman period by philosophers such as Lucretius; and Pyrrho of Elis, the founder of the extremely influential school of scepticism. And for a later example, we have Plotinus who came up with a new version of Platonism (now called 'Neoplatonism'), which was extremely influential on the Italian Renaissance more than a thousand years later. We should also not forget the formation of Christian theology. Many of the key figures in the early church were very accomplished philosophers indeed; Augustine stands out.

In fact, you are rather unlikely to come across any of these on a first-year course (with the possible exception of Augustine). But you might see mentions of these names, or the philosophical movements to which they belonged, in your reading.

With the exception of Anselm's ontological argument, and Aquinas' versions of the cosmological argument, you are also unlikely to see any medieval philosophy on your first year. This may be even more unfortunate than the highly selective approach to ancient philosophy discussed above. Many students get through university believing that nothing much of interest happened in the medieval period. And nearly a thousand years of marvellous philosophy gets forgotten.

Sample essay on Plato's 'Phaedo'

Question: Critically discuss the purpose and validity of the 'final argument' in Plato's *Phaedo* (2,500 words).

Plato's dialogue *Phaedo* is about the last hours of Socrates' life. In it, Plato treats three inter-related themes: the philosophical life and death; the nature of change and permanence (and thus the question of the permanence or immortality of the soul); and the existence and importance of forms. The 'final argument' is the culmination of these three themes such that the soul is proved to be immortal because it is akin to the forms, but in such a way as to require 'care'. This 'care' is the philosophical life, as a preparation for philosophical death.

In order to discuss how this argument works, we must first look very briefly at two previous arguments from earlier in the dialogue: the cyclical argument and the recollection argument. These arguments first introduce ideas important for understanding the final argument. Then, we will turn to the final argument, and try to explain its key terms and features, before concluding that the argument is incomplete.

[Notice this introduction is quite brief – it addresses the context of the question in a couple of sentences, and then sketches the important divisions within the essay in another couple. This may seem a little bit bare or arid to you, and it is. But this student only has 2,500 words, and she hasn't got time to be elegant, or to wander off on side-tracks.]

The first argument we need to consider (the 'cyclical' argument) is at 70–2. Socrates is trying to prove the immortality of the soul. If the soul is immortal, then the philosopher need not fear death, and there may even be sense in additionally claiming that the philosophical life consists in preparing the soul for death. Briefly, in this argument Socrates first says that opposites come from opposites. For example, 'if something smaller comes to be, it will come from something larger before, which became smaller' (71). This seems quite reasonable: for example if I get rich I must have been not-rich (i.e. poor) before. He then says that life and death are opposites, and since from life death follows, so in the same way from death life must be produced. I agree with Carerra, who argues that Socrates is just playing around with words (Carerra 1974: 39). That is, he is falsely equating the meaning of 'comes from' in 'death comes from life' and 'larger comes from smaller'. This overlooks the possibility that death might simply be the ceasing to exist of life, instead of a change from one opposite to the other. Life might be a property of the body, instead of a thing – and the objection Simmias makes at 85e–86d is precisely this point. In reply, though, Socrates claims to prove that the soul must be different from the body, a thing in its own right, and this becomes one of the premises of the final argument (Jeremies 1989: 119).

[*This is only a brief account of this argument, for it is not the main focus of the essay. Obviously, if you were writing mainly about this argument, you would be expected to go into more detail. Notice how it is made clear exactly why it was important to mention this argument in an essay that is about a different part of the dialogue. Finally, notice two things about referencing. First, references to the texts of some philosophers (Plato, Aristotle and Kant, to name three) are not references to the page numbers in the translation you happen to be using, but are references to a standard pagination of the original language. All translations will key into this standard pagination. Second, notice how referencing to secondary sources is done: fully, but quickly.*]

In the 'recollection' argument, Socrates says that truths cannot be attained by the bodily senses. Rather, it is our intellect or reason that 'lays hold' of things as they really are. What he is getting at are Ideas or Forms, such as Equality or Beauty or Goodness. The forms are something like eternal, unchanging and ideal objects which serve as our mind's means of grasping ordinary things which, in themselves, are constantly changing and never perfect. He tries to prove that we must have knowledge of these forms or else we could not possibly have knowledge of ordinary things (such as sticks that are equal in length). (It is unnecessary to pursue the details of Socrates' argument at this point.) Since knowledge of the forms is required for knowledge of the world, we couldn't have learnt these things after our birth, after, that is, we entered this world. The only other possibility is that we must have learnt them before birth. And therefore 'we' in some sense must have been around before we were born, and therefore our souls must be immortal.

[Why is the 'f' in 'Forms' sometimes capitalised and sometimes not? Either would be acceptable, but not both. A minor detail, perhaps, but the kind of thing thorough proofreading should have caught.]

This seems a very confusing argument. It doesn't prove quite what Socrates wants it to prove. It proves, at best, that souls were around before birth, not that they will *continue* to exist after death and in fact be truly immortal. Cebes' objection – that the soul might 'wear out' – is related to this kind of problem. However, importantly, Socrates has made a plausible case for the existence of forms as ideal things that are eternal and unchanging. What seems at first like just part of an argument to prove something else (that the soul existed before the body was born) will turn out to be much more central. Again, this account of the forms becomes one of the starting points of the 'final' argument (Jeremies 1989: 117).

[Again, the student has not really gone into Socrates' argument at all. Instead, she has merely made clear its relation to the immortality of the soul problem, and to the existence and significance of the forms. In fact, this student really could have done without supplying criticisms

of this argument and the previous one. The only criticisms that would be necessary would be ones that help to clarify the contribution the earlier arguments are going to make to the later one (the real focus of the essay). As slimmed down as it looks, this essay could be even leaner!]

The final argument seeks to overcome all of those defects which are partially represented in the dialogue, as we've said, by the objections raised by Simmias and Cebes. What Socrates wants to prove is that the soul brings life to the body, and that the soul is the kind of thing that can never admit the opposite of life, that is death. Therefore, the soul may leave the body for dead, but itself is immortal.

[This is an introduction to the last part of the essay. Very brief, its purpose is simply to orient the reader.]

The Forms seem to have opposites: hot, cold, large, small, just, unjust, life, death. It is quite clear that the Forms never 'admit' their opposites: the large can never admit the small. When the small comes, the large must either give way or perish. While Socrates has already tried to prove that things come into being and perish into their opposites, the same cannot be said of the opposites *themselves*, the forms. If the form of cold itself perished, then nothing could ever be cold again!

But now Socrates posits an intermediate level, between forms and particular things; Socrates never calls them 'forms'. Burns (in an interpretation she admits is 'controversial') calls these things 'form-like things', and said they might be interpreted as something like what philosophers such as Descartes mean by substances (Burns 2000: 49). That is, types of existence which have distinct and above all essential, fixed properties – that is, an essential, fixed relation to a particular form. Fire is one of Socrates' examples. Fire is not the opposite of snow. Form-like things are not themselves opposites to anything. But when fire enters a particular thing, it brings with it a form which does have an opposite, hot. Moreover, because it always brings with it a form that has an opposite, fire must yield to cold (the opposite of hot) whenever cold arrives – or, for that matter, to snow (another 'form-like thing' which always brings with it cold, the opposite of hot). It is not just hot that yields to cold, but fire too, insofar as when it enters a thing it necessarily brings with it the hot. Plato believes these 'form-like' things allow him to give real explanations of why things change, rather than the 'ignorant' (105c) explanation that something is hot just because of hotness. Thus, the plausibility of positing the existence of such things is that such a hypothesis is both consistent with the recollection argument in general, but also allows a real understanding of the world: to say that illness is caused by the opposite of the form of health may be true, but pointless; to say it is caused by a fever might be useful.

[*The first steps of the argument are explained by defining what, in the student's analysis, a 'form-like thing' might mean, and by analysing one of Socrates' own examples. Always define key terms, and don't let examples explain themselves if there is any possibility of confusion. Notice that she has not chosen to lay out the argument as a list of steps; instead, she has chosen a slightly less informal way of presentation. There are advantages and disadvantages to both methods. The list form makes it clear how the parts of the argument are separated, but it can be a problem indicating how they are supposed to be related. The ordinary paragraph form is good at relations, but not so good at separation. In both cases, in other words, you need to be careful, clear and complete. Notice that the plausibility of these steps is discussed: the discussion of this argument is going to be much more complete than for the preliminary arguments above.*]

The soul is such a form-like thing, according to Socrates. It brings with it to the body the form of life, and being a thing can in principle leave the body. But because it carries within it the form of life, it cannot admit the form of death. Therefore, it is immortal. However, unlike a form, a form-like thing has a direct acquaintance with ordinary things (wood can have a direct acquaintance with fire; similarly, the body, in which the soul resides). This direct acquaintance can be threatened (the body could be poisoned), but can also threaten the 'purity' of the form-like thing. The necessity of care for the soul, which Socrates expands upon in the mythological passage at the end of the dialogue, seems to follow from this fact. Socrates says, 'Those who have purified themselves sufficiently by philosophy live in the future [after death] altogether without a body' (114c). What exactly Socrates is saying is not very clear in this dialogue, but certainly some kind of close relation is suggested between the three themes: philosophical life, immortality of the soul, the forms.

[The student here allows herself an apparent digression on care for the soul. This is apparently incidental to the argument itself, but is important to the student's general thesis about the final argument gathering together all the themes of the essay, and also directly relates to the idea she suggests in the conclusion about why the final argument had to have been left incomplete. So it is not really a digression: perhaps, though, she could have put in one more sentence making clear what she is up to.]

However, this is not quite as strong an argument as it might seem. Even if we accept the hypothesis of the 'form-like things' (which is not proved but only at best plausible) there is still another serious problem. All it says is that an *existing* soul can never have the *property* of non-life. It does not also prove that an existing soul can *never not exist*, that is, that it is indestructible. Indeed, Socrates goes out of his way to emphasise that none of the other form-like things (fire or threeness) are necessarily indestructible – when confronted by snow, fire must either get out of the way, or perish. So we cannot assume that the soul is indestructible, that is, necessarily gets out of the way, rather than perishes. This stage of the argument passes very quickly: Cebes seems to say that if there is anything that is indestructible, then that which is immortal must be. Or, the reverse: if even the immortal is destructible, then everything else must be. But this is not yet an argument: what exactly is wrong with assuming that *everything* is destructible? And Socrates seems to reinforce Cebes' point by adding that there are, indeed, deathless or immortal things which are indestructible things: God and the form of life itself (106d). Again, no argument, just a couple of (rather dubious) examples. We have to conclude, therefore, that the final argument, despite a promising start, is incomplete.

> [This is the 'critical' discussion part. It raises two objections to the argument. This is good: any more than two, and the discussion of the objections might have been too quick and thin. Notice that this paragraph is nicely framed by an opening sentence that announces the question of whether the argument works, and a brief concluding sentence that summarises the conclusion.]

For this reason, I conclude that Plato does not in fact prove that the soul is immortal. The previous arguments in the dialogue are not acceptable proofs in their own right, but simply contribute important ideas to this final argument, and the latter is quite badly incomplete. But perhaps that is the point. One of the themes of the dialogue is the philosophical life, which seems to be a life of questioning, and striving after a proper relationship with the forms, and thus care for the soul. By leaving the 'final' argument incomplete, Socrates is ensuring that his friends and followers must continue to live the philosophical life. They cannot simply rest with the simple and reassuring knowledge of the soul's immortality. Thus, at the end of the final argument, Socrates slyly asks: 'And so now, if we are agreed that the deathless is indestructible, the soul, beside being deathless, is indestructible. If not, we need another argument' (106c–d). In other words, the dialogue when considered as a teaching device, as an incentive to philosophise, in short as a model of the philosophical life itself, requires that questions remain to be answered (Hugh 1989: 36). This incompleteness of the *argument* about the immortality of the soul is, in fact, part of the *procedure* of the care of the soul.

> *[Introducing new ideas in the introduction is slightly dangerous and normally not such a good idea. If something is important, it should be in the main body of the essay; if not, it should not be included at all. The conclusion, basically, should be pretty much a restatement of what your thesis is, and (briefly) a sketch of what you have done to demonstrate it. However, it can be a good idea to discuss the* significance *of your thesis, and/or where it is might eventually lead as a philosophical problem – and this is something like what this student has done here.]*

BIBLIOGRAPHY

Burns, D. (2000), *Forms and Things in Plato* (London: Sonority Press).
Carrera, Sarah (1974), *The Immortality of the Soul* (New York: Macmillan).
Jeremies, Jerry E. 1(989), 'The Structure of Plato's *Phaedo*'. In Peter Paterson (ed.), *Plato and the Dialogue Form* (New York: Vintage).
Hugh, D. (1989), 'Writing and philosophical Activity in Plato'. In Peter Paterson (ed.), *Plato and the Dialogue Form* (New York: Vintage).
Plato (1977), *Phaedo*, trans. G.M.A Grube (Indianapolis: Hackett).

Hobbes, Thomas (1588–1679) Hobbes is primarily known as a political philosopher. He attempted to make politics into a science by trying to discover the basic principles according to which any political association must function, which in turn is based upon a 'scientific' analysis of how human beings think and act. The scientific aspect was largely based upon *materialism*, the philosophical (ultimately metaphysical) position that holds that the only existing thing is matter in motion, and that all events can be explained as effects of matter in motion. The attempt to thoroughly carry out the implications of this position is Hobbes' other great contribution to philosophy. First-year students may also encounter Hobbes' discussions of the free-will problem, or his contributions to the 'Objections and Replies' that followed Descartes' *Meditations*.

2.2.7 Early modern philosophy

While Medieval philosophy is only rarely encountered on first-year courses, you'll find it difficult to avoid 'early modern philosophy'. By 'early modern' here I mean from the late sixteenth to around the middle of the eighteenth centuries. The names that you are most likely to encounter are Descartes, Hobbes, Locke and Hume.

This period is so frequently taught for at least two related reasons. First, the philosophical concerns of, say, Descartes seem to more closely resemble the concerns of recent philosophers. In other words, these figures set the agenda for philosophical enquiry over the next few hundred years. Second, the language, style and outlook of a philosopher like Locke, for example, are more recognisably modern (and thus more accessible to the reader today) than a medieval or ancient philosopher. The problem with stressing 'modern philosophy' so strongly in the first year of your degree is that it becomes difficult to avoid the conclusion that Descartes et al. 'got it right' about what philosophy is supposed to be trying to achieve, and how it is supposed to achieve it. Often, the next couple of years of undergraduate study must then try to undo this overly simple and complacent conclusion!

You may come across a first-year course that is about nothing but this period (and, indeed, may be called 'Modern Philosophy'), this would be a 'historical' course according to the typology of course we discussed in section 1.2.3 'Typical philosophy courses' above. Or, there may be a course that is about nothing but *one* of these philosophers (a text course). But more likely, you will strike upon these figures in courses on other topics: Descartes on a course on metaphysics or the philosophy of mind; Locke and Hume most likely on an epistemology course; Hobbes in political philosophy. Keep in mind that the purpose of historical and text-based courses is quite different from a problem course, and thus the nature of the discussion and of assessment will probably also be different. For example, if working through Hume's *Treatise* is a

Locke, John (1632–1704) Locke was one of the most
significant of that group of philosophers called the 'empiricists'.
Locke's major work, the massive *Essay Concerning Human
Understanding*, is a systematic attempt to show how every
aspect of understanding of reality (such as complex ideas about
time or causation) can be traced back to reflection on ordinary
sensible experience of the world alone, and that we need not
assume any nonsense like 'innate' ideas along the way. He was
also concerned to show that such a derivation of our ideas (1)
was fully compatible with the most successful scientific theories
of his age – above all Newton's – and (2) helped to solve a
number of philosophical problems that other philosophers had
been unable to solve (for example, the nature of our personal
identity). Locke also makes important contributions to political
philosophy, with one of the earliest and most influential
discussions of the concept of 'rights'.

chief part of the purpose of the course, then you will be
expected to try to grasp what Hume really meant, and to
that end evaluate a number of possible interpretations of his
text. On the other hand, in a problem-based course we tend to
be less interested in what Hume *really* meant, than how
something he *apparently* thought might help us to analyse
or solve a problem.

A sample examination paper for a fictional first-year course
on Descartes is given in Part Two of this book, in the section
on examinations.

2.2.8 'European' or 'continental' philosophy

There are a number of philosophers after Kant who tend to be
read together as part of a certain loose tradition of doing
philosophy. Such a grouping will probably include Hegel,
Kierkegaard, Nietzsche, Sartre and so forth. (The last two
of these names sometimes show up on first-year courses in
philosophy.) It is to this tradition of philosophy that the names

'European' or 'continental' philosophy refer. There is another loose tradition, which includes figures as diverse as Mill, Russell, Ayer and Wittgenstein, that is usually called 'analytic' philosophy, and sometimes even called 'Anglo-American' philosophy. What are we to make of this?

First of all, and very sadly, this distinction has political importance within philosophy. Someone calling themselves 'analytic' or 'continental' can, for that reason, be automatically excluded from serious consideration by the other tradition. At several philosophy departments in the UK, such tensions go right through the middle of the department. Such divisions are hardly unique to philosophy, however. As professions, history, English and psychology (naming only three) are equally divided. A rats-in-mazes experimental psychologist, for instance, might well find laughable a colleague working in the psychoanalytic tradition of Freud.

Second, it is important to note that these designations are not terribly good as *descriptions*. Many eminent 'continental' philosophers are English or American; many eminent philosophers who live in France or Poland, say, would probably call themselves 'analytic' philosophers, and it may even be the case that 'analysis' strictly speaking is not a terribly important part of their work. Calling someone a 'European' philosopher, then, is a bit like calling a restaurant 'French'. The restaurant does not have to be *in* France, the chef does not have to be French or have been trained in France – and snails do not have to be on the menu either. To make it even more complicated, there are an increasing number of philosophers who refuse to be located in either tradition, or who use elements of both in their work.

Third, other than by starting with the above idea of a tradition of philosophers, it is very difficult to pin down exactly what 'continental' philosophers do that is always different from what 'analytic' philosophers do. The most common negative stereotypes around are that 'continental' philosophers are interested in making improbably grand statements on the basis of merely subjective affections, poorly understood science, or dubious political and social theory, and generally writing in a deliberately obscure and often paradoxical style. Or, that 'analytic' philosophers blithely assume that the structure of any logic is unequivocally capable of capturing the structure of language, thought or the world, and otherwise are so interested in fine logical distinctions that they completely miss the important philosophical wood for the trivial conceptual trees. It's probably best that we say no more on this subject, and thus avoid repeating such gross over-simplifications and caricatures.

Most philosophy departments offer at least some courses on both types of philosophy (you may even encounter a course that tries to do both at once). In departments dominated by 'continental' philosophers (of which there are only a handful in the UK), the 'analytic' offerings might be little more than tokens, and correspondingly the reverse in 'analytic'-dominated departments. There is nothing wrong with such 'tokenism', since it at least shows a professional interest in providing you with a broad and inclusive education. However, you might want more. So, if on the basis of previous reading or study, you are confident that 'analytic' or 'continental' philosophy is for you, then you should look out for, and avoid, such tokenism when choosing which university to study at, and which courses to take.

PART II
Study Skills in Philosophy

3 BE IN THE KNOW

3.1 INTRODUCTION

You cannot settle down to study effectively unless you know what you are doing and why you are doing it. At all levels – what you are doing with your life, what you are doing at university, what you are doing in a philosophy class – the more informed and aware you are, the better will be your motivation and your ability to study. This introduction aims to take some of the worry out of daily life at university. Do not be surprised to find, among the information on study skills, a number of hints on what might be described as life skills. For the time you are at university, the two are inextricably linked.

'Learning to learn' sounds like a daft slogan, but it's actually an important part of what you can hope to achieve while at university. Indeed, throughout your time at university, you will be required to reflect upon and evaluate your own learning. For example, all universities are now introducing 'Progress Files'. Part of this file you will write yourself, on a regular basis (like a kind of thoughtful diary) concerning the progress you have made in acquiring subject-specific and general skills. Don't worry about this, it's not assessed, nor will it be arduous. But it does indicate just how important is your ability to understand *how learning happens*. That is why, in the following, I will rarely just tell you what's a good thing to do. Instead, I try to explain why it's a good idea to get into the habit of conducting your learning in certain ways.

3.2 BE IN THE KNOW ABOUT YOUR SUBJECT

3.2.1 The class/course booklet

As part of your degree, you will take a number of individual courses in philosophy – and each one runs slightly differently. Thus, most courses have a course (or 'class' or 'module') booklet with essential information such as course content, reading lists, a timetable, what the assessment procedures are, whether or not you have to register for exams and, if so, where and when. The course book may also tell you how essays and other written work should be presented. Always read the class booklet carefully, and refer to it from time to time, just to remind yourself of what you should be doing at any given point in the term. There may also be a booklet covering the general structures and procedures of your whole degree/award.

3.2.2 The noticeboard

Find out where the department noticeboards are and keep a regular eye on them. Any changes to class times and locations will be posted there, sometimes at short notice. It is the place to look for tutorial lists, exam details and so on. Also important will be notification of visiting speakers, philosophy society events, and so forth.

3.2.3 The office

Various departments organise themselves in different ways. The role of the departmental/school office may vary, but it is always important. In some universities, for example, the departmental secretary keeps all the handouts for lectures. In some universities, your essays are handed into the office. The office is normally the place to go if you want to double-check dates and places for exams, if you can't get hold of a particular lecturer, or if you change your address and so on. The departmental/school office may not be open to student enquiries all day. Find out when the secretary is available.

3.2.4 Computing support

Even if you are a complete technophobe, you must find out how to make the most of the available computing facilities. Increasingly, university departments insist that written work be done on a word processor. Some even ask for work to be submitted in an electronic form so that it may be scanned for plagiarism.

On a more positive note, a word processor makes editing and revising your work very much easier; you have the benefit of a spell checker, and you produce an attractive final copy, which will put the marker in a good mood.

There will almost certainly be brief courses on computing for new students and they are well worth going to, whether you are computer literate or a complete beginner. You will save a lot of time and effort if you find out how much your computer can do for you. Even if you know your way around computers, you can still learn a great deal about, for example, the software available, how user names and passwords are allotted, how the network printers are used, and so forth. Computing-support personnel are patient, and equally good at helping nervous beginners and more adventurous, technically minded users.

The computer is also essential for gathering information from library catalogues and from the Internet.

You will probably be given an email address in your first week. Check your email frequently because this may be how your tutors, lecturers or the departmental secretary will get in touch if they need to contact you urgently, and it will be appreciated by your tutor if you send an email if you have to miss a class. Moreover, there may be a way that you can send an email to every other student on one of your courses – this will permit you to continue tutorial/seminar discussions out-side of class, and is strongly encouraged.

Before you even apply to a university, explore the websites of universities you are considering. They might help you to decide which university to chose.

4 LEARNING AT UNIVERSITY

4.1 READING

Your lecturers will recommend reading to be done along with the lecture course. Some will be assigned on a lecture-by-lecture and tutorial-by-tutorial basis. You will get the most out of the lectures and the reading if they keep pace with each other. Frequently, there will be minimum required reading for a lecture course (for example, a course on Descartes' *Meditations* will undoubtedly require you to read it!), but there will almost certainly be additional reading so that you can broaden your knowledge of the subject and assess different points of view.

Your first task is to get hold of the book or article. There will be some texts that are recommended for purchase and, knowing that students are always short of money, lecturers will keep this list to a minimum. Watch the noticeboards for second-hand copies, explore local used bookshops, or consider using second-hand book sites on the web. If you are tempted to buy an old edition, check with your tutor that there have not been too many changes. This is relatively unlikely in philosophy, but, on the other hand, getting the required translation of a foreign-language text can be very important (there are dozens of translations of the *Meditations*, for example).

Books that you do not have to buy will be in the library. Make sure that you are first in the queue. There are always more students than books. Right from the start, get to know your library and how it works. Get to know the shelf numbers where philosophy books are kept. In philosophy, this can be a bit tricky, since, for example, political philosophy and metaphysics will be in quite different locations. Practise using the on-line library catalogue, which at many institutions can be accessed off-campus via the web. The catalogue will tell you not only where to find books, but also whether they have been borrowed and when they are due back. If a book that you need has been borrowed, you may be able to recall it, or reserve it. Just ask at the service desk.

Many important texts in the history of philosophy are available on the web, for free. However, your tutor may still want you to use paper versions, both because they are easier to get on with in class and because the tutor will know that they are of good quality. So, for required reading, its best to buy in the bookshop – but for extra reading, by all means use the Internet. For example, you may need to buy a particular version of Descartes' *Meditations*, but your reading of that book will be much enhanced by reading other things by Descartes, and you can find these on line. Many on line versions have nothing like page numbers, so, for referencing, you must go by chapter/section number – that is, the inbuilt structure of the book you are reading.

In the library, there may be more than one place to find books. For example, there are the ordinary open shelves (or stacks) that make up most of the library but, in addition, especially when books are recommended for essays and there is likely to be a huge demand for them, books may be put in a special section of the library where they are on very short loans, say three hours at a time. There may also be a special collection with rare or valuable books, and a reference section with dictionaries, encyclopedias and so forth. If you have problems, the most valuable resource in a library is the librarian. Ask a member of the library staff for help.

For more information on finding sources, please also see section 5.1.6 below, entitled 'Finding and using sources'.

Before reading anything, sit back for a minute and ask 'Why am I reading this?' – in other words, 'What questions do I hope to find answers to?' Maybe you are reading to prepare for a seminar, and you have been given topics or questions that go with that particular day's seminar. Or perhaps you are reading in order to write an essay on a particular question. In either case, keep the questions in mind while you read.

The best academic writers, particularly those who are directing their writing towards first-year students, try very hard to keep their writing clear and easy to read. However, it is not always possible to express very complex ideas in very simple language. Furthermore, learning a new subject means learning all the terminology of that subject. Thus, occasionally, some of the reading that you do will be very dry and difficult. Persist. Gradually, you will build up your reading muscles to Olympic standards. This is yet another of the benefits of a university education: no act of parliament, company report or small print on a contract will daunt you after graduation!

In philosophy, none of the reading you will be doing is exactly bedtime-story stuff. It demands what is called 'active reading'. You really have to work and think along with the text. For this reason, do not underestimate how long a chapter will take and do not set yourself too big a chunk of reading in one sitting. Apart from the introductory chapter of each book, you are unlikely to be able to read a chapter straight through from beginning to end. Take it a bit at a time. In philosophy textbooks, there will often be exercises or questions to think about; do these as you go along, it will really help reinforce your reading. If there are no exercises, set yourself some!

As you read, look for the following:

- What appear to be definitive statements of position. The author might even help you by writing *In summary* . . . *In conclusion* . . . But that will not always be the case. These statements are likely to be the conclusion to an argument.

- What evidence is supplied in support of the conclusion? Look for key examples and analogies upon which the author is relying. Think of other examples, and ask whether they work in the same way. Are there counter-examples that don't seem to work? (Write down your observations, and raise them in tutorials/ seminars.)

- Look also for (hopefully) logical arguments that progress step by step and lead to the conclusion. Are these arguments valid? Are any dubious assumptions being made?

- Look for places where the author is talking about some other philosopher, or philosophical topic, about which you might know something. This can be a good way into understanding what the author is on about, and can also be a good topic for the tutorial/seminar. Write down your observations and take them to class.

- Look for relationships with other topics you are studying. If your reading is for week five of a course, ask yourself how what you are reading connects with weeks three and four, and even how the topic of week six might follow. Write these connections down; they can be excellent topics for discussion in the tutorial/seminar.

- Jot down questions for tutorials/seminars. For example, 'This passage seems to be important, but I didn't understand what X means by . . .' These needn't be questions, of course. If you think something is up with the philosopher's argument, raise it.

- Take notes. Try to rephrase the text in your own words as you do so. Occasionally, joint study sessions with other members of your tutorial group might be helpful. Together, you might make more sense of difficult passages, come up with good examples, or be able to test each other.

The moment you sit down with a book, make sure you note down all the necessary bibliographical detail (see section 6.2.1 on referencing and bibliographies below), including page numbers. As you take notes, make sure to indicate the page from which each paraphrased or quoted idea comes from. Be sure to indicate in your notes that exact quotations are not your own words. If you find something you may wish to quote word for word, make sure that you get every detail right, including the punctuation. If it contains what looks like an error, put '[sic]' after the error and then everyone will know that you are quoting accurately and the mistake is not yours.

For more advice on good note-taking, see the bit on making notes in the section 5.2.4 'The writing process' below.

Only once you have done the recommended reading should you start looking for additional reading. The set books might make recommendations, or you could browse along the library shelves, or you could do a search on the library on-line catalogue. Subject searches are not always reliable. Some-times keywords in the title can produce better results. This might produce such a wealth of material that you don't know where to start. A good guide is the number of times a book or article is cited in other people's bibliographies. You will see from this which texts are important reading. If you need help, ask your tutor. Once you have found a few secondary books that look relevant and useful, use their bibliographies as the starting point for further searches.

When you are browsing, use the contents page or abstract to identify useful and interesting bits and skim-read for key terms to find the bits you want. Do not start at the beginning and try to work your way through. First make sure that the book or article has something to offer.

Sometimes, you will come across references to books, or articles in academic journals, that are not held by your library. It is normally possible to order them by 'inter-library loan'– ask your librarian about the procedure for this.

If you want to photocopy anything, you must obey the regulations on copyright displayed beside university photo-copying machines.

4.2 LEARNING BY ASSESSMENT

There are two kinds of assessment, formative and summative. A formative assessment will be due in the middle of the term or semester; it counts towards your final mark but it also, and even more importantly, provides you with the feedback you need to improve your performance and get the most out of the course. The summative assessment is the final appraisal of what you have learned during the course.

The most usual ways of assessing student performance in philosophy are essays and examinations. There may be a small proportion of marks for tutorial participation. Most institutions now use continuous assessment, which means that early, formative work counts towards the final mark.

Exams and essays usually give a generous amount of choice; you can choose to answer a question from a list of five or ten. This practice can leave a large part of the course unexamined in any way. Therefore, some course organisers prefer to set assignments that require short answers to questions, thus covering a much greater proportion of the course curriculum. These assignments are not necessarily set under exam conditions but might take the place of a class exam. All the comments in the chapters on 'Examinations' and 'Writing clearly and correctly' apply equally well to assignments.

Whatever form your assessed classwork takes, the marks are for your benefit as much as for the examiners' benefit. The class booklet should tell you what the marks really mean in terms of whether you have just passed, or passed well, or passed outstandingly. Go by what the class booklet says rather than by comparing yourself with other students. Some years seem to produce a larger number of good students than other years, but the marking criteria stay the same. Look at the markers' comments, good as well as bad, and try to see what makes a good philosophy answer. If a few of you can get together and go over marked essays, exams or assignments, you will get a better picture of what markers are looking for.

4.3 SELF-DIRECTED LEARNING

This is the main difference between studying for your A levels at school, and university study. You will be required to spend less time in a classroom, and accordingly more time studying on your own. *A great deal more time*. Good self-directed study habits are a key difference between a successful university student, and one who struggles.

Libraries are usually good places to work, if you can manage to ignore occasional, irritating whisperers. You are less likely to fidget and go off to do other things than you are at home. You are not going to be distracted by flatmates, visits to the fridge or your favourite television programme. Your library will have hundreds of study places where you can work for hours, close to your source materials. Try also to get into the habit of using the library in breaks between classes, potentially useful time which can easily be frittered away.

If you live with other students, make sure that there are clear rules about not interrupting each other's study time. People who play very loud music at three in the morning before a flatmate's exam are not appreciated. Be considerate about your flatmates' exams and essay deadlines and make sure they do the same for you.

By now you will be aware of the length of time that you can work without a break. You are unlikely to be working effectively if you go for much more than an hour without a brief rest. You can keep your concentration up for longer if you vary your tasks. For example, read and note-take for a bit, and then go back over your notes and imagine writing a short exam answer on the subject. If there are practical exercises associated with the subject (as there will be for logic), then do one or two of those, before going back to reading again. Again, remember not to set yourself too much reading in one go.

Sit down to study with a realistic target in mind. Reward yourself (with a rest, a cup of tea, a chat with friends or a phonecall) when you have achieved your goal. Try to avoid working late at night; this can adversely affect your concentration in class the next day. If you find that this is becoming a habit, revise your time management. If you do find yourself burning the midnight oil, and all students do from time to time, strong coffee or other highly caffeinated drinks are probably not the answer. At least not every night.

4.4 TIME MANAGEMENT

Time management is one of the transferable skills that employers value in a university graduate.

As you progressed through school, you will gradually have been given more and more responsibility for your own time management but, between school and university, there is a great chasm. You were expected to get to school at the same time every morning and stay there and work until everybody went home. If you were not at a class, somebody wanted to know where you were. Homework was given in comparatively small, regular amounts and woe betide you if it was not done.

At university, you may not have a class every day. You may start at nine in the morning, but you might not re-start until the afternoon. The strict routine of school disappears. You have to make sure you establish a good new routine. Bad time-managers start getting up late, missing classes, working late to try to meet deadlines and end up feeling permanently tired, miserable and inadequate. Time management starts when the alarm clock goes off. You need to establish a daily routine.

You also need to keep an eye on the bigger time-management picture. If you were a course organiser, how would you work out the deadline for handing in essays? You can't set an essay too early in the course because the work has not been covered. You want to hand marked essays back in time for students to learn from them before the exams. All course organisers think this way and so the deadlines for essays for all your subjects have a nasty habit of falling around the same time. It is no excuse to say, 'I had three essays to hand in for today. I haven't finished my Greek Metaphysics one. Please can I have an extension?' That will simply not be accepted as an excuse. The time between the setting of the essay and the deadline is very generous, perhaps as much as five weeks. The time to get started is as soon as possible after the essay topics are given out. Furthermore, being quick off the mark means that you get to the library before all the books on the reading list disappear. The best cure for poor time management is an early start.

Keep a calendar with *all* the due dates, and *all* the examination dates in it. This will allow you to see immediately how much time you have for writing essays and exam revision. Use the calendar to divide up the time between your courses; perhaps colour code each day. Stick to this plan – and when you do, each day, give yourself a little reward. If for some reason (like illness) you fall behind, don't just scramble to catch up. Instead, re-plan all your courses, dividing up your time as it now seems to you to be necessary. Never plan to finish an essay on the due date. Always give yourself at least that last day in case of disaster (my printer is out of ink!).

Some subjects you can swot up the week before exams and use flair or common sense to fill in the gaps. Philosophy is not one of them. Exams in philosophy are designed less to see if you know some facts about Descartes, than to test your *understanding*. This understanding takes some time and patience to acquire – longer than a week! This doesn't mean that the exams are really hard, though. If you keep up with lectures and tutorials, and do required and recommended reading, you will find the exams are really not a problem.

You can improve your exam technique greatly by planning how much time you are going to spend on each question and sticking to it. You know the duration of the exam and you know the number of questions. Assuming that each question is worth the same number of marks, you simply divide the time equally among the questions. This may sound obvious, but it is amazing how many students make a mess of exams because they don't do it. Over-revising for one of several questions is a bad strategy.

In the examination hall, time management is still important. The question paper may ask you to write on three questions in two hours. That's forty minutes each. Keep your watch by your side, and stick to the forty minutes, because in general you will get more points for two slightly sketchy answers than for one completed answer and one blank. Also, as you write an exam answer, you pick up marks very rapidly in the first ten or fifteen minutes of writing. After that, the rate at which you collect marks slows down and eventually you reach a plateau.

There may even come a point when you end up exposing your ignorance instead of showing off your knowledge and your marks could begin to drop. For essay-type answers, note the time at which you must start to draw each question to a close. That is, give yourself five or ten minutes to write a conclusion to your answer. Even if you have not completely finished when your time is up, move ruthlessly on to the next question. You may have time to go back and finish it later. Often, each answer is written in a separate book, but, if this is not the case, leave a big space between answers so that you can go back and add any necessary finishing touches. If there are questions which are divided into sections, work out how much time you can afford to spend on each section and pace yourself accordingly. If you have practised on past papers, you may find that there are some questions you can do quite quickly. When it comes to the exam, do the quick ones first and divide up the time you have saved among the remaining questions. (For more on examinations, please see section 5.2 below.)

If you have had to get a job in order to pay your way through university, keep your priorities clear. University comes first. When you start missing classes to go to work, something has gone wrong. Both the university and the Students' Union will have officers trained to help you through financial difficulties.

Finally, remember to plan some time for relaxation. If you deliberately leave time for having a bit of fun, then you will not be so tempted to let your relaxation time eat into your working time.

4.5 TUTORIALS AND SEMINARS

The various scheduled hours for learning at university can be divided up into three types. First, lectures, which tend to be relatively big groups in big rooms. In lectures, the learning is one-directional: the lecturer tells you things, you listen, think and write them down. Second, tutorials, which are probably the most efficient and enjoyable way of learning. They usually consist of a small group of students and a tutor. The focus is normally on two-way discussion of the ideas in the lecture. In some departments, a 'tutorial' is defined as one-to-one with a tutor. Third and finally, the seminar. This is a rather vague term because different teachers (and different departments) approach seminars in different ways. Some treat them as large tutorials and others treat them as small lectures. Be aware that some departments/universities use the term 'seminar' instead of 'tutorial' to mean 'small group of students in discussion with tutor'.

Right from the beginning, get to know at least some of the people in your tutorial group. It can be a great help to go for coffee after a tutorial and talk about philosophy with people who are at the same stage as you. It means that you will have people you know to sit next to in lectures. It also means that if for any reason you have to miss a lecture, you can borrow lecture notes easily. Finally, if you are all strapped for cash, you can even share the purchase of books. (Be careful if sharing library books, though. The person who takes them out is responsible for their return, no exceptions.)

The better prepared you are for a tutorial, the more you will get out of it. Obviously, you should do any reading assigned for that session, and go through your notes from the lecture. Write down questions and comments that arise during this reading and bring them to the seminar. (See section 4.1 on 'Reading', above.)

A tutorial/seminar group has many aims: (1) to reinforce lectures; (2) to clarify any points in the lectures or the reading that you did not understand (3) to give students practice thinking 'on the fly', talking about philosophy, and debating issues rationally; (4) and to explore topics in more depth than can be attempted in lectures, perhaps moving on to related topics that were not covered in the lecture but which are still relevant to the course. Accordingly, there will be a variety of opportunities for you to contribute. These include, roughly corresponding to the above: (1) opportunities to ask questions of the 'Can you explain that again?' type, concerning the lecture or the reading; (2) there will also be opportunities to comment on lectures and reading ('I think I've found a counter-example . . .'); (3) there will be a chance to participate in debates among the students concerning how an idea should be understood or evaluated (these can get quite lively and even heated); these debates may be open, in which everyone contributes and tries to back up their own views on the matter, or they may be 'staged' where the whole group is divided into teams that debate one side of an issue; (4) finally, your tutor will keep things moving towards his or her objectives by asking questions of the class ('Why does Descartes produce this argument at this point?). Thus, to get the most out of a tutorial, you need to tell your tutor where your difficulties and interests lie, and you need to be *active* in tutorials, or else the whole thing won't work for anyone concerned. The best way to overcome shyness (if you need to) is to be prepared: do the reading, and write down questions or comments in advance. That way, you don't have to worry about formulating what you say in front of people. Obviously, this will be most pertinent to (1) and (2) above, although what you've written may well be a good contribution to debates and new questions. You should steel yourself for an impromptu contribution as well.

However, do not be afraid of asking something silly or giving a wrong answer. This is easier said than done, to be sure, but having something to say is always useful, both to yourself and to the group as a whole. In tutorials, you are very unlikely to be assessed on what you know (although you should clarify any criteria for assessment with your tutor); that's the job of essays and examinations. If tutors award a mark for tutorial performance at all (and not all courses have tutorial assessment) it will be based on attendance and participation. If you make a mistake in a tutorial, you and your tutor can get to the bottom of it and clear up any misunderstandings. That's participation, and it's what your tutor wants. Your tutor may even thank you for noticing an ambiguity in the lecture. Better to make a mistake in a tutorial than in the exams or essays.

By the same token, you should deal respectfully with your

fellow students. This means: don't hog the seminar. If you have lots to say, that's good, but try to pick only the gems. Don't interrupt or talk over someone else. And above all do not belittle someone if you think they've got it wrong. In the heat of a debate it's difficult not to sound dismissive of another's proposal, but you must try. The whole learning process will work better for *everyone* if each behaves him- or herself. Do not be surprised if the tutor introduces a 'learning contract' which makes the above rules explicit.

Don't forget that the particular topic under discussion is only part of what a tutorial is about. You should also be paying attention to how your tutor addresses him- or herself to philosophical problems: careful use of examples, construction and evaluation of arguments, and so forth. This is your chance to learn how philosophers *do philosophy*.

Attendance at tutorials is almost always compulsory and if your attendance is poor, the tutor will be obliged to inform the course organiser and your director of studies or personal tutor. This is partly for academic reasons, to make sure you are not falling behind with your work. It is also for pastoral reasons, to make sure you are not ill or in some kind of difficulty. Please try to let your tutor know if you are going to be absent. Because tutors are the members of university staff that students come into contact with most frequently, they are often the first person that a student will consult about a non-academic problem.

If you have any special needs, tell your tutors if there is anything they can do to help. For example, if you are partially deaf and need to lip read, suggest to the tutor that you sit where you can see the tutor's face clearly, in good lighting, and ask the tutor to help by speaking clearly. If the tutor lapses and starts talking to the blackboard, a quick reminder will be appreciated.

If you are stuck with your essay, seek help from your tutor. Do not expect any help that would give you an unfair advantage: don't ask your tutor to come up with your ideas for you, or tell you how to write out your ideas, exactly what to read so that you don't have to spend some time in the

library, or what your mark will be! Your tutor is not there to
save you work, but to help you see the strengths and weaknesses of the work you have already done, and thus help *you*
to realise what your next steps must be.

In the last tutorial before the exams, keep your ears tuned in
for clues. Your tutor may be authorised to tell you a bit about
the exam layout. You may go over old papers in the tutorial
and be given hints on question spotting or hints on structuring
answers. If the course has changed recently, past papers can
put you in a complete panic by asking about things you have
not covered, and your tutor will be able to reassure you. If the
tutor does some exam revision with you, which topics are the
focus of attention? After the exam, be sure to ask your tutor
about any mistakes you have made if you cannot see for
yourself how to put them right.

4.6 LECTURES

First-year philosophy classes can be quite large. A certain
amount of noise is inevitable, particularly during the winter
term when everybody seems to have coughs and colds.
Coughs, inexplicably, get worse during lectures. Therefore,
it is a good idea to arrive in good time and get a seat quite near
the front where there is less chance of being distracted and you
will be able to hear. If the lecturer is inaudible or if the visual
aids are not visible, let the lecturer know at once. If you have a
hearing problem, consult the university's special needs advi-
sor. If you have a motor or visual problem and cannot take
notes, ask the lecturer if you can use a tape-recorder. Tape-
recorders should not be used by anyone without permission.

Lecturing styles vary quite a lot and so you must be able to
adapt your note-taking and listening. Most lecturers provide a
course outline in the class booklet and it is a good idea to take
a look at this and get a general picture of where the lectures are
heading. Some lecturers follow a published book (sometimes
their own). Also, you may well get a handout at the lecture or
handouts may be collected in a class booklet. If there is such a

class booklet, make sure you take it with you. If the lecturer sticks closely to the handout, it might be enough just to make marginal notes on it. If there is no handout, or if the handout is extra to the content of the lecture, be sure to take notes. You may think you will remember it all but you won't. However, you won't be able to write everything down – instead, you will have to think about what is being said in order to record the basic idea quickly and accurately. That is why the lecturer doesn't just give you a transcript of the lecture: lectures are meant to stimulate you to think and understand, not just to transmit information!

A good lecturer will have planned the lecture and it will have a structure. In fact, even although the lecturer may sound quite spontaneous, the lecture should have been constructed in sections and paragraphs like a well-thought-out essay. The lecturer may tell you the game plan at the start of the lecture. Try to structure your notes accordingly. Use bullet points and numbers where possible. Consider using a different coloured pen (or just large asterisks in the margin) to highlight key terms and important points. This will help with exam revision. You would be very exceptional if your concentration did not lapse occasionally in lectures, but train yourself to waken rapidly if the lecturer gives any signals such as saying, 'Let us try to define this term . . .' or 'The key argument here is that . . .'

Just like in tutorials/seminars, part of the purpose of a lecture is for you to see a philosopher in action, irrespective of the content of the lecture. The structure of a lecture, for example, or the care taken in defining a position, should be models for your own work. You should be aware that some lecturers and tutors prefer a 'Socratic method' where they explore an issue as if for the first time, without disclosing their own views. Others may say up front something like 'I believe that X. How can we show this to be correct, or incorrect?' – or perhaps even pretending to a belief for the sake of argument. What's important is that the discussion after is open: your lecturers do not expect you to agree with them, unless and until they make a good case for their views.

Not all lecturers are charismatic and riveting, but don't

confuse a drier style with poor content. Nevertheless, you may have to make a big effort to stop your attention from wandering. On these occasions, you could try active rather than passive listening. Imagine you are in a radio discussion programme and you are going to have to respond to what the lecturer is saying. What can you agree with? What would you question? What stimulates you to think in fresh directions? Not only will this game help to keep you awake but it will also help you to take good notes.

Always take a look over, and make sense of, your lecture notes the same night (preferably in a group), while the lecture is still fresh in your mind and, if there is recommended reading to do, do it as soon as possible after the lecture. An excellent idea is to revise your lecture notes with a friend, in the hope that your wandering moments do not coincide and that if one of you has a gap in your notes, the other can supply the deficiency. By the same token, if you miss a lecture, borrow notes for the same lecture from at least two people.

The series of lectures that make up a course may be divided into topics, blocks or modules. Make a special effort to get to the last lecture of each of these topics. This is when you might pick up hints about exam questions.

5 ASSESSMENTS

5.1 ESSAYS AND DISSERTATIONS

You did not get as far as considering university entrance without having gained some skill in writing, but learning to write well is a life-long task. During your time at university, you will be expected to polish your formal writing style and adapt to the particular conventions of the discipline you are writing about.

At university, you will be assessed primarily on what you write. But this 'what' is inseparable from 'how' you write, because it does not matter how much you know if you cannot get that knowledge down on paper in a way that makes sense to the reader.

Learn from your successes and your mistakes. If you are about to write your first philosophy essay, read on. But if this is not your first, first go back and have a look at the marks and comments on previous work. What general good and bad things lay behind those marks? Also, think about how you prepared for that essay: what did you need more time for, how did you take notes and did that work out, what aspects of writing gave you most trouble, and so forth? Where there was a problem consult the appropriate section below for useful advice. (See section 5.1.5, 'The essay returns!', below.)

Make the most of available technology: this can make writing and revising an essay much easier, and is virtually essential for doing research. Many university departments insist on the use of word processors for essays.

5.1.1 Why write essays?

From one point of view, because they are required! That is, in order for you to pass the course, your tutor needs to have proof that you have learnt something. But that is a narrow, 'official' point of view. If you tackle your essays in the right way, you will find that they are, in fact, a very important part of the learning process. It is only when you try to explain things in a totally clear and unambiguous way that you begin to expose little gaps in your understanding. So you have to consolidate your learning. More encouragingly, you may find that, as you arrange your ideas, you make connections that you had not seen before. You are putting what you have learnt to work and gaining confidence in handling your new knowledge. The more effort you put into an essay, the more you will benefit.

Essay writing at university level demands knowledge of the conventions of academic discourse and especially of the way of writing accepted within your particular subject. All academic discourse demands attention to detail, not just in the facts and theories you present, but also in the manner of presentation. A consistent level of formality is required and an impersonal style where the writer does not get in the way of the subject. Vocabulary and grammar have to be carefully checked to make sure there is no possibility of misunderstandings. Sources have to be cited and listed in a bibliography. You are handling complicated ideas and having to express them clearly. In short, you are becoming an expert in the transferable skills of gathering, selecting, organising and communicating information. Writing essays is not just about getting good marks in your subject, or even learning your subject well. It's also about mastering a set of skills not specific to philosophy that will serve you for years after your time at university is finished.

Do not be surprised if some of your courses/modules require short essays in the middle of the teaching term, instead of or in addition to some assessment at the end. This is designed to help you consolidate your knowledge and improve your skills as you go along. Indeed, you may even be required to submit drafts, summaries, or essay plans of your work. In this way, tutors try to ensure that you do not leave things to the last minute, and are also able to give you valuable guidance on both the content and form of your work.

5.1.2 Philosophy essays are different

(1). Different subjects are written about in different ways. This is partly because of the differing nature of subjects and partly as the result of traditions and conventions. Literature essays, for example, are usually written in continuous prose; history essays are too, although there may also be a need to include visual evidence or tables of data. Science and technology essays will be interspersed with formulae, data and graphs. A philosophy essay tends to be more on the continuous prose end of this spectrum, but occasionally a diagram can be useful, or a few formulae from formal logic. For any type of essay, the emphasis is always on clear, effective communication.

As you can see from the first part of this book, philosophy embraces topics of very different kinds. Some of them lend themselves to a quite black-and-white, factual approach – for example, if you were required just to explain what Descartes meant in a certain passage, or just to lay out the classic arguments for and against a moral thesis. This can be exacerbated by some topics. Imagine an essay that was discussing the moral issues surrounding global warming. It might be necessary, in order to evaluate the utility of certain approaches to the problem, to lay out data concerning projected harvests, or sea levels, in a table. Other topics allow for more discussion – for example, a question that asks you to evaluate an argument, or discuss the relation between two ideas. Still other topics will require a slightly different approach again. Imagine, for example, an essay looking for philosophical ideas about nature in a Shakespeare play. Such an essay would have to pay attention to the language in the play in a manner different to an 'ordinary' philosophy essay.

The point of this discussion is that the overall style of a

philosophy essay has to adapt itself to the subject, but, again, the emphasis must always be on clear and effective communication, and on *constructing a justified answer to a question*.

(2). This idea of constructing a justified answer to a question is the key to philosophy essays. More important than the above comments about style is the fact that philosophy essays are (almost without exception) 'argumentative' essays. That is, their purpose as essays is to try to demonstrate the truth of a claim by the use of argumentation. As you will see in section 5.1.4.1, 'Finding a structure', below, this is how we will introduce the whole idea of writing a philosophy essay.

It is sometimes said that, in philosophy, your answer is never right or wrong. This is, at best, only partly true. Insofar as part of the task of writing an essay is showing your understanding of a philosopher's work, and writing clearly and carefully, then you certainly can get this very wrong. Again, insofar as part of the task of writing an essay is to attempt to justify a conclusion, then – if your supposed justification was an invalid argument, or obviously insufficient evidence – you can also get this very wrong. What is meant by the 'never right or wrong' is that for every philosophical position however cherished, there is always the possibility of a rational objection to it. But the objection has to be rational, and that means not based upon misinterpretation or a bad argument.

(3). You may be surprised to discover that, at least in the first year of a university course in philosophy, students are not expected to be particularly innovative. There is a lot of groundwork required before you are ready to produce original work. Occasionally, students are worried because they feel they are not writing anything new but just reproducing what they have heard in lectures and read in books and articles. The issue, however, is not whether you are having new ideas or not, but whether you are doing a *little more* than just 're-producing'. In particular, good essays demonstrate an ability to handle, apply and in general understand the knowledge.

What the marker is looking for is the ability to work with the information, to select the bits that answer the question, to put them together in a meaningful way, and to evaluate their significance and validity. If you can do all that, you are demonstrating an understanding of the subject. Where you can use creativity and originality is in your selection of examples to illustrate the points you are making. If your examples are apt, the marker knows you have understood the concepts you are illustrating. You should also not under-estimate the level of creativity required just to make a complex idea or argument clear and understandable.

Occasionally, you are encouraged or required by your tutors to work on an essay-like project in a group with other students. Please see section 5.3, 'Oral presentations', for some relevant additional advice.

5.1.3 First, read the question

In advance of writing the essay, perhaps weeks in advance, you will be given a question paper with a list of essay questions from which you must choose. Sometimes, it will be a list of one, so there is no choice involved. And at other times, your tutor will want you to have a hand in inventing an essay question for yourself. This is especially true in philosophy, where the skill of formulating an interesting question is valued as highly as the skill of providing an answer. If this is permitted, you should always clarify the exact wording of your question with the tutor. For your tutor's experience will quickly identify questions that it will be very difficult, maybe impossible, to answer in the space provided.

More good students get bad marks because they have misread the question than for any other reason. Make sure you undertake the activity asked for. Similarly, everything you write must be relevant to the question. If you include irrelevancies, they will not gain marks and they will even lose marks by taking up space that should have been used on answering the question. Word limits on essays are based on the assumption that every word is necessary and to the point. If you are in any doubt what an essay question means, do not be afraid to ask whoever set it. Questions do not appear in isolation. You may have been given guidelines or criteria. Consult these as carefully as you do the question!

So, what's involved in picking a question? Within each question, you should notice three elements:

1. A set of what-to-do words, such as 'compare', 'evaluate', or 'discuss'. These are important: if you compare when you are asked to discuss, you may lose points. These words break down to a number of key activities:

   - First, 'explain', 'explicate', 'describe', 'give an overview', and so on. Here, you are being asked to give a straightforward restatement of a position or argument, in your own words, in as much detail as you can, and being as faithful to the thinking in the original as you can. This will involve, for example, defining the key terms used, and laying out the structure of the argument. For example:

     In his study of tragedy, Aristotle attaches considerable importance to the concept of 'catharsis'. Provide an overview of three interpretations of what Aristotle might have meant by this term.

   - Note that rarely in philosophy will you be asked only to 'explain' or 'describe' a position. Rather, you will be required to go a step further and 'evaluate', 'analyse', 'give a critical account of', 'discuss', 'assess', and so on. Here, you are being asked to determine the validity and soundness of a position or argument – to what extent you believe it to be true, and why. You may also be asked to consider the implications of its truth or falsity. Now, doing all this, you will probably have to perform a task of the first type as well (i.e. 'explain', 'describe', and so forth) in order to get to the point where you can evaluate. It's important to remember that being 'critical' does not mean to 'be negative', any more than all film critics hate all films. Instead, it means to evaluate objectively and rationally. So, if you are asked to 'critically analyse' an argument you could go on to agree entirely with it, but you will have discussed and rejected various objections, and perhaps have come up with additional reasons for agreement. For example,

> Evaluate three interpretations of what Aristotle meant by 'catharsis'.

- Third, 'relate', 'compare', 'show the relation of' and so on. In these cases, you are being asked to take two different positions/arguments – perhaps from different philosophers, or from the same philosopher in two different places – and show what connections there may be. This might involve, for example, arguing that these two positions actually amount to the same thing, although they use different words. (Or different things, although they use the same words.) Or it might mean showing how one philosopher has influenced another. Or, finally, it might mean showing how a philosopher's ideas in one part of his or her work lead on to ideas in an apparently unrelated part of his or her work. In any case, you again will probably need to do work of the first ('explain' etc.) and perhaps also the second type ('evaluate') on each half of the comparison. For example,

> 'Aristotle was unable to agree with Plato's rejection of poetry because of an underlying metaphysical disagreement.'
>
> Discuss.

Notice that this question has a slightly unusual form. It begins with a quotation (which the tutor may have just made up) that expresses a particular opinion, and asks you to interpret the quotation, and agree or disagree with it. You may come across this form of question frequently. This question is an example of this third type of question because, clearly, the quotation suggests a *comparison* of Aristotle and Plato.

- Finally, 'apply', 'solve', 'consider', 'suppose' and so on. You are being asked to apply your analysis of a certain philosophical position to a real or hypothetical new problem. For example, to ask how a moral theory might work out in a particular applied case, or how does a slightly bizarre thought-experiment change our understanding of epistemology. It's as if you are being set a puzzle to solve, using the resources you learned in class. To solve this puzzle you will certainly need to do work of the first two types above. For example,

  Suppose there were a transportation device that could take your body, analyse it down to the last atom, send the analysis to another location where an exact duplicate of your body was formed from raw materials. The original body is then destroyed. Would the being that stepped out at the other end be *you*? What implications does your answer have for our understanding of our personal identity?

2. The second thing to notice in questions is a topic or set of topics that determine the basic issues you will be writing about. For example, the question might include 'Descartes' and 'imagination' and 'Fifth *Meditation*'. Your essay will need to address all of the set topics.

3. You may also find some structural hints. For example, the 'transportation device' question is strongly pushing you towards an essay in three consecutive parts.

For further discussion of the kinds of questions that philosophy students are commonly asked, please have a look at section 5.2 on 'Examinations' below, which includes a discussion of a sample paper.

Having carefully considered the question, you will now have a strong sense of what is being asked. Remember you are answering a particular set question: so it is a good idea to start by imagining what an answer to the question must be like. What topics must it consider, what questions or issues must it address? Based just on what you know now (from lectures, assigned reading, seminar discussion), how would you tackle the question? This will lead you to a list of important considerations: what kinds of things must you deal with in order to cover the question, and arrive at an answer. These important considerations will map (approximately at least) on to the 'points' or 'steps' of the body of your essay. And this, in turn, should lead to a *rough plan or outline*.

The essay you are writing is part of the assessment for a particular course. What are the aims of the course, what are its 'learning outcomes'? In short, what is the tutor expecting that student will know or be able to do? These things will be what the essay is supposed to be evidence for. Just as your tutors will design courses backwards from the outcomes, so you can understand what the essay questions are asking for by working backwards too. Of course, it's dangerous to second-guess your tutors too much – and, in any case, your tutor is not out to trick you with the essay questions. Nevertheless, looking at the question from the point of view of the tutor's job of assessing the outcomes of the course can be enlightening.

5.1.4 The writing process: from notes to a first draft

You've chosen the question, and had a think about what it is asking, and what key topics must be discussed. What next?

Writing is not a single big task. It is a lot of little tasks:

- finding a structure;

- collecting information;

- making a draft;

- polishing;

- preparing for submission; and

- proofreading.

5.1.4.1 Finding a structure

First, we need to talk a little about what essays are supposed to do. An essay (*especially* a philosophy essay) is an attempt to **construct a justified answer to a question**. What does this mean?

- 'Construct': this means that an essay will be made up of more than one part, and that these parts have to work together for the essay to be successful. The essay will begin with an introduction, it will end with a conclusion. In between is the 'body' of the essay, itself made up of several parts. Let us call the various bits of the essay's body the 'points' that you, the author, wish to make.

- 'Justified' means that coming up with an answer (even a 'correct' answer) is not enough – you must work out why your answer is a good one. So, what does it mean to say that your answer is a 'good one', that the conclusion you arrive at is 'justified', or that one point 'follows from' another? These are ways of describing how arguments work. Arguments are the backbone of any philosophy essay. As you progress in philosophy, you'll get very good at working with arguments, large and small. That is a key reason for studying logic, after all. But for the briefest of introductions, see section 6.1.1 on 'Critical thinking'.

- 'Answer to a question': essays are normally written in response to a question set by your tutor. Some are clearly questions, for example, 'How successful is Descartes' version of the ontological argument?' Others are discussion-type questions, which invite you to formulate your own thesis on a topic. For example, 'Discuss the role of imagination in

Descartes' sixth *Meditation*.' In such a case, it is always a good idea to begin by thinking of a *question* which best represents your views on the topic. For example, you might decide to ask yourself, 'Does Descartes have a coherent theory of the imagination in the sixth *Meditation*?' or 'What is the relationship between imagination and the body in Descartes' sixth *Meditation*?' Thinking about the topic in terms of a question will get you thinking about your essay in terms of *answering* a question. The more clearly you can pin down an exact question – the more your essay has a *clear theme or main idea* – the better. Such a clear theme will then act as a filter, helping you determine what kinds of things should go in your essay, and what stuff you can leave out.

Students are usually surprised at how much importance markers attach to the structure of essays. Anybody can re-gurgitate a bucket of facts. From the above, you can already see that that is not what essay writing is about. Markers are looking for understanding, or the ability to put the facts to work, in order to construct a justified answer to a question. In general, you are expected to construct some kind of argument. In this context, argument does not necessarily mean anything confrontational. It simply means that your essay should have a thread running through it, such that everything in the essay contributes to answering the question asked, and contributes in a way and an order that is clear to the reader.

Sometimes the wording of an essay title suggests a structure: *Explicate and critically discuss Kant's first argument for space being a form of intuition. Why is this argument important to Kant's broader position?* This question suggests a three-part essay: first, an attempt to lay out, as clearly as possible, what Kant had to say; second, an evaluation of its success as an argument; and, third, locating the particular argument in the context of Kant's philosophy.

Don't forget that philosophers are keen on definitions, and for good reason. The above question, for example, would probably require you to define what Kant actually meant by 'form' or 'intuition'. A warning: definitions from ordinary dictionaries (as opposed to specialised dictionaries of philosophy) are rarely any good here. Furthermore, some words ('form' is a good example) receive completely different definitions by different philosophers.

If no obvious structure suggests itself, experiment with different ways of writing an essay plan. Below are some possible methods.

Some people use mind-maps. Put the core idea down on the middle of a bit of paper and let other ideas branch off. These other ideas might be sub-topics suggested by the structure of the question you have been asked (as in the example below). Or, they might be aspects of a particular issue: for example, in the sample examination answer on Kant in part one of this book (2.2.5), the mind-map might have had 'moral argument' in the middle, and 'practical', 'theoretical' and 'possibility of moral action' as branches. In turn, these secondary ideas might generate their own branches. Little clusters may start to form. These might each form a section or paragraph of your argument. If a similar idea crops up in two places, ask yourself if that produces a possible link between sections.

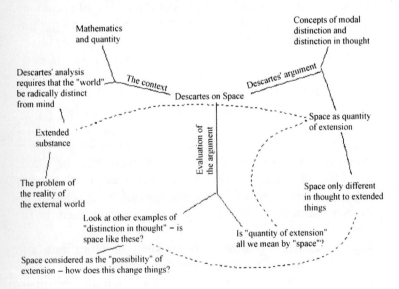

Figure 5.1   Mind-map for question on Descartes' metaphysics of space

Figure 5.1 is a simple mind-map for the following essay question: *Discuss the context and validity of Descartes' argument concerning the separate existence of space.* Mind-maps are great for breaking down complex ideas into simple parts, and showing the interrelationships between ideas. In Figure 5.1, we used solid lines in order to analyse an issue (such as defining what exactly is Descartes' argument) into its parts, and we used dashed lines to indicate important relationships. In the completed essay, these dashed lines would be references from one section back to a previous section.

After completing the map, you would then need to decide upon an order to write these ideas. You would need to ask yourself: which comes first, or stands most obviously on its own? That is, which of all these ideas can be written about clearly without having to assume all the other ideas? That will probably be the first section of your essay. In the above case, the best order is pretty clear: context, argument, evaluation. For other essays, it may be more difficult to decide on a good order.

You might prefer a more hierarchical plan, such as this sort of outline form (for an essay on Kant's theory of intuition):

1. *Kant's argument*
   a. *definitions of key terms*
      i. *'form'* . . .
      ii. *'intuition'* . . .
   b. *what is the argument supposed to demonstrate?*
      i. . . .
      ii. . . .
   c. *what are the argument's key assumptions?*
   d. *the structure of the argument*
2. *Evaluation*
   a. *X's criticism*
      i. . . .
      ii. *How might Kant have responded?*
   b. *Y's criticism* . . .

And so forth. You might wish to use such an outline *after* having a go at a mind-map. This will help you to move from the analysis and connections you have discovered in the mind-map, to determining how an essay will look on the page.

For certain kinds of essays, for example an essay on applied ethics, you might try listing the pros and cons of a position, as if it were a calm and unhurried debate between two opposed views.

All these strategies may uncover such possible orders as: a logical progression as a proof unfolds; a movement from the general to the particular, perhaps stating a hypothesis and testing it on specific examples; or moving from the particular to the general, constructing a hypothesis from the evidence you have set out.

If no plan emerges, do not despair. Sometimes the act of writing brings the necessary insights. Get started on freewriting. To do this, just write as fast as you can, without stopping to think, without lifting your pen, for at least three minutes. It doesn't matter if you write nonsense. At least you have something on paper to expand, re-order and improve. If you still cannot see a way of making all the information hang together as a whole instead of a jumble of facts, seek help from your tutor.

5.1.4.2 Building up a structure

Introduction	Body: Point one	Body: Point two, etc.	Conclusion	Bibliography
Orients your reader towards the philo-sophical work that follows.	This is the first step on the road to your con-clusion.	Second step towards the conclusion, etc. Don't forget to make clear what the relation is between this point and one preceding it. That is, how you get from point one to point two, from point two to three, etc.	The conclusion states your answer to the question asked and normally also summarises the reasons you feel your answer is justified.	This is a list, in the standard format given below, of all the resources you actually used in the preparation of your essay. *Where* you used these sources will be indicated by 'references' throughout your introduction, body and conclusion.

Figure 5.2 A typical essay's structure

INTRODUCTION

The first part of your essays is the *introduction* (see fig. 5.2). Your introduction explains what the issue or topic is that you will be discussing; it may also include a bit of context on the topic which helps to bring out its wider significance. In brief essays this context should be kept to a bare minimum, or even eliminated, unless the instructions for the essay ask you to include it. The introduction should include a kind of brief summary of what follows, since it will help your reader to follow your essay. You could state your objectives, or list the main issues you intend to deal with (in the order that they appear in your essay), or say briefly what you intend to explain or discuss. If the 'question' you have been assigned is just a bare topic, without a clear question, then a good way to tackle the opening paragraph is to phrase it as a question, into your own words, say what you understand by it, and prepare your reader for the way you are going to answer it.

In very brief essays, of one or two pages, this introduction should probably be no more than three or four sentences. In longer essays, you have a bit more breathing space to introduce the topic. In this opening paragraph, you want to get the reader interested. In this case, a good introduction would find a way to show the importance or significance of the topic, the problems it addresses, or the implications it carries. For example, 'There is considerable urgency to Descartes' writing in this passage. If he cannot sustain his argument, he has good reasons for believing that a total scepticism would be unstoppable.' But don't run the risk of writing 'filler', such as irrelevant contextual information, instead of getting down to work.

BODY

This is the main portion of the text, in which all the various aspects of the topic are discussed. In Figure 5.2, the body is broken up into 'points' or 'steps'. For example, your first point may be a careful definition of one of Descartes' key terms. The second point may explore an ambiguity in Descartes' use of this term, with references to various of his texts. The third may detail Descartes' argument for the truth of one of his key ideas.

The fourth might consider a different interpretation of the argument that you found in a secondary source, and the reasons why your interpretation is to be preferred. You should keep your reader apprised of what you are up to. So, when you finish one point, you should mark the transition to the next, perhaps by writing something like 'Having looked at the problem of X, we will now turn to the problem of Y, because . . .' For some advice on how to make these connections and transitions clear, see 'Good academic style' section 6.2.2, below.

It almost goes without saying that you should always do one thing at a time: discuss a definition, lay out an argument, and so on. This shows clarity of thought on your part, and helps your reader to follow the thread of your essay. It is a common weakness in student essays to dive into the middle of a problem, dealing with key definitions, arguments and implications all in a muddle. Good advance structural planning should prevent this.

Note that in long essays (1,500 or more words), the points in your main body can usefully be seen as mini-essays, each of which has a brief introduction of a sentence or two, a main body (with sub-points) and a one-sentence conclusion. Each mini-essay would deal with an aspect of the larger problem you are investigating. For example, arguing for a particular way of understanding a key term; analysing the meaning of an important example or analogy; explicating what is going on in a brief textual passage, etc. The structure would then look like Figure 5.3.

Introduction	Body: Point one	Body: Point two, etc.	Conclusion	Bibliography
	Introduction	As 'point one', but		
	Body:	including forwards		
	Sub-point a	and backwards		
	Sub-point b	explanations as to		
	Sub-point c	how the various		
	. . .	points fit together.		
	Conclusion			

Figure 5.3 Structure of the main body of an essay

In this way, your essay always keeps a tight, clear structure. Everyone, including you, knows exactly where they are.

CONCLUSION

Finally, the conclusion. Again, in very brief essays, this should be no more than a few sentences, and should make explicit how you have answered the question asked. For example, if the question is 'Has Kant successfully proved X?', your conclusion might say: 'We must conclude that Kant's argument for X is sound. For, as we have seen above, all of the premises and assumptions Kant needs can be justified, and the conclusion follows logically from these. Moreover, we have defended a Kantian response to Nietzsche's objection that Y...' In longer essays, the conclusion again can be slightly more elaborate, perhaps discussing the wider significance of your specific conclusion, or mentioning points that deserve further consideration. Try to avoid mechanically repeating the question you have been set and the way you answered it.

5.1.4.3 The process of writing

The first sentence is always the hardest! But it's a lot easier if you've prepared the ground, by doing some decent background work, and by finding a workable structure.

Writing is a process with a number of identifiable steps. You have already decided on a question, and (based mainly on lecture notes you already have) begun to develop a structure that should lead from the question to its answer. What comes next?

READ THE QUESTION CAREFULLY

We've already talked about that above. And don't forget guidelines or criteria, which may be in different documents.

FINDING A STRUCTURE

We've done that, too. You should now have something like an outline of the main sections of your essay.

GATHERING RESOURCES

You need to collect information that will help you to fill in this provisional outline. This means gathering relevant resources: if the essay is about Descartes, say, you will obviously want to reread anything in Descartes that might be relevant. Much of the information you need will have been covered in lectures and reinforced in tutorials. A good essay, however, always shows signs of additional reading that has been well understood and used appropriately. Indeed, it may be a requirement of your work that it is adequately researched, in which case not doing this additional reading, and not using it, will lose you points.

Please also see section 5.1.6, 'Finding and using sources', below.

This kind of information collection will happen at three separate stages in the writing of your essay. First, perhaps even before you seriously consider the structure of your essay, you will need to review your notes, reread the primary textual passages, and perhaps have a quick go at some introductory level books on the subject just to help you to get oriented. This is called 'background research', and should help you get clear in your mind what basic concepts are going to be addressed, what the main issues are, and what are some of the alternative approaches that can be taken to problems.

Then, after you have put together a provisional structure and done some light background research, you need to do the 'real' research. You'll want information and arguments that help you to discover and back up your position, but you'll also want information or arguments that differ from your position and with which you can critically engage. Finally, in the course of actually writing up the essay, you may discover a point that is unclear to you, or something that didn't seem important at first may turn out to be crucial. In that case, another trip to the library will be needed.

Tutors are often asked, 'How many books/articles should I use in writing my essay?' It is an impossible question to answer, because it depends upon the question you are asked, and the essay you are expected to produce. For short essays in your first year, it may be that two or three sources are sufficient for you to get good marks in that area. This will not be sufficient for longer essays, however. (Also one source is never enough, because the resulting essay is likely to end up skewed.)

MAKING NOTES

Why are you taking notes? Because the book is due back in the library tomorrow, perhaps. But even when you have a copy of a book or article to keep, taking notes is still important. If all you do is underline or highlight passages, how will you know the week after *why* you considered them important, and *where* they fit into your plans? Taking notes on your sources is an important intermediate stage between just 'reading up' on a topic, and composing an essay (or an examination question, for that matter). The fact that note-taking is already on the way towards composing a possible essay gives you the 'why'. *You are taking notes in order to answer questions.* Make a list of what you hope to find out, and keep it in front of you while reading and note-taking. This will keep you focused and alert. You can, of course, add to the list while reading – that shows you are reading actively.

Some people like to read a text through completely, and then *immediately thereafter* skim back through it to take notes. Others prefer to take notes as they read. The first method probably produces better quality notes; the second is more reliable, especially if you are vulnerable to distraction!

Much of your note-taking will consist of paraphrases or summaries of the text, but often a passage from a book will spark off your own ideas. Make a note of the passage and write down your responses to the passage at once, or you will almost certainly forget what they were. Notes are an aid to learning, not a substitute for it. You should not just copy down quotes for future reference. Try to take notes in your own words. Before you can do that, you have to understand what you have read and that is the first step in learning. The physical act of writing something down will help to fix it in your mind. Also, you have to be selective and, in being selective, you begin to exercise your critical judgement. If you then take *notes of your notes*, you repeat these learning steps. If you are using your own book or a photocopy, you will probably use highlighter pen. Do not be tempted to use highlighter or underlining as a way of not having to read something that you suspect is important but is too hard to understand. Make the effort then and there. If it is important enough to highlight, it is important enough to learn. Do not highlight indiscriminately or you will not be able to see the wood for the trees.

Also, your purpose in taking notes on a particular text may differ. On one occasion, you may just be looking for help interpreting one particular idea, and that's it. Anything else the author says will not be of any use to you. At other times, the author may be writing on exactly your essay topic, and you need to engage with every word (although, of course, you'll probably not use all this in your essay). Also, there's always the possibility of surprise: something you thought would be of only limited use turns out to be central! That's part of the fun of doing research.

Pace yourself in note-taking. Don't try to do more than one article or book chapter in a row. Separate the jobs by reading a bit of the primary text, perhaps, or just take a short break. If you are tired, you are more likely to lose your focus and take notes that are not relevant to the question.

As mentioned above, when taking notes keep the essay question (and any other sub-questions you need answers to) in front of you. Constantly ask yourself, 'How does what I'm reading relate to the question?' This will mean that your notes are not just summaries or quotes from the book, but will also include your own comments, such as 'this will help me to define what Descartes means by X' or 'nice argument – I'll need to address this' or 'I don't think this example works because . . .' This will also keep your note-taking relevant to the question, and not too exhausting. Don't forget, you are not *copying out* the book, just taking notes *for a particular question*. Noting down your reactions to what you are reading can also be a good way of getting into the actual writing of your essay.

Make sure that in your notes it is always clear where the idea is coming from, and whether it is a direct quote or your own wording. This may seem tiresome, but after the first time you lose track of a reference and have to spend a desperate couple of hours in the library trying to find it again, you'll learn. Even more dangerous is putting something from your notes into an essay that you *think* was your own idea, but is actually a quotation from a book you read. Why dangerous? Because you can be accused of, and failed for, plagiarism. (See section 6.2.1, 'References and bibliographies', below.)

Since academic writing demands that you provide proper bibliographies listing all the works you have consulted, it is particularly important that you record *all* the necessary bibliographic details (see below). If you take something off the Internet, make sure you record the website and the date you accessed it. With an internet site, you should also travel up the hierarchy of the site in order to find out who produced it, and for what purpose. There will be a huge difference in the credibility of a site produced by a university (look for the .edu or .ac suffixes on the web address), compared with something bunged on to the Web by a fourteen-year-old! Obviously, the same warning applies to material found on a discussion forum, chat rooms, or email lists.

Please don't write in library books: it costs the university library precious resources. Only if you are using your own books or photocopies are highlighter pens acceptable! Also, remember not to break copyright rules when you are photo-copying. The rules should be clearly displayed near the university photocopiers. If in doubt, ask a librarian.

RECONSIDER YOUR PLAN

So, you have a provisional plan, and now several sets of notes. Clearly, you should keep revising your provisional plan, as new discoveries and new ideas change your approach to the question. As a new idea pops up, you may also need to go back (probably to the library) and gather more resources, and research them. Your aim here is to get a plan that answers the question set for you by your tutor, and uses that question as a *clear guiding theme* throughout (and thus does not include irrelevant points, or useless background material). With a bit of luck, by the time you finish the first big note-taking stage, your plan will have evolved into something quite plausible and clear. However, don't worry if your plan and its question or theme isn't looking completely clear just yet. Sometimes a philosopher only figures out what they want to say in the middle of writing – or even after! Still, though, working on your plan will keep you focused.

In order to test further whether your plan is going to work out, you need to start filling in the gaps. You need to start writing.

STARTING WRITING

It might seem a good idea to begin by writing out the introduction. But that is not always true. If the question asked is pretty clear as to what is required, then there's no point writing the introductory paragraph first, since you already have a good idea how you are going to proceed. Many writers work on the introduction *last*, since they don't know exactly what it is supposed to be introducing yet! On the other hand, if the question is not entirely clear what it wants, or if your essay plan still feels a bit vague, then you could try starting with the opening paragraph. This would involve writing about the question, putting it into your own words, saying what you understand by it and what kind of an answer you will giving (not *what* the answer is, because you may not know that, but *what kind* of answer: e.g. a discussion, an evaluation, an explanation, etc.). This should help you tighten up your plan as well.

If you are having difficulty getting started, remember that you do not have to start at the beginning. It is always a good idea to get some 'exercise' writing, to become used to handling the relevant vocabulary. Some of the ideas that you have jotted down while reading and note-taking can be written out to form a series of nuclei around which you can build up your text. If you wrote, for example, 'this example is misleading because . . .', develop that criticism up into a paragraph. Such paragraphs will at least be a serious start, and may well slot neatly into your planned structure.

A similar technique for starting will be to work on the 'expository' passages. That is, material that merely explains something else, without yet evaluating, discussing or contextualising it. For example, in regard to the essay discussion topic given above, you might have a go at explaining what Descartes seems to mean by 'imagination'. Or you might try to lay out briefly what the context of your topic is (what problem the sixth *Meditation* is apparently trying to solve). Or, if there is a brief piece of text you are focusing on, try to write a paragraph that simply gives an exposition of that text, putting it into your own words in such a way as to make it extremely clear. Doing this kind of writing is also a good way of spotting problems you might not have noticed otherwise. Again, such paragraphs may form parts of your finished essay. If the words still will not come, try talking. Explain what you are trying to write (just the one issue) to your flatmate, your cat or your bathroom wall. However bright the cat, it probably doesn't understand – be clear and patient. Write down exactly what you said.

If you write more than one expository passage, or more than one paragraph based on an idea you put in your notes, keep each on a separate sheet of paper or index card (or put several spaces between them on the word processor). Then, later, you can rearrange them as needed. If you tend to write straight on to a word processor, a smaller window can be less intimidating than a huge blank screen waiting to be filled.

Ideas are like buses – either none come or they all come at once. So, when you have plenty of ideas, just concentrate on getting them all down. Whether you use a word processor or pen and paper, just enjoy the experience. Worry about spelling, grammar and the exact words later. An essay that overflows with ideas and has to be cut down and refined is better than one that has to be padded out.

WRITING IT OUT
You've now got a plan that seems to hang together, and maybe some expository writing. All you have to do now is write your

essay out in its full form! Write a first draft. Here, there are broadly two techniques. First, write the briefest of introductions, stating what you think is really the issue at stake, and then put down in order the series of points you feel you need to make, and don't forget to help your reader by making clear how you see these points as 'adding together' in order to get somewhere. Second, forget the introduction; instead, write the briefest of conclusions first and then work backwards through the points needed to reach that conclusion. In either case, don't be alarmed if your essay summary (and the plan behind it) needs to change as you write and discover new problems or issues that need to be addressed. Keep your plan flexible. What you write may give you new inspiration. You may find connections you had not noticed before and you may need to revise your essay plan a bit. It is very easy to move chunks of text around on your word processor; experimenting with structure is not a problem. However, when you move text around, make sure that the seams don't show. Read it over to check that the section you have moved links into its new surroundings.

One good reason for writing *both* the introduction and the conclusion last is that producing these forces you to stand back from your work, and consider its overall coherence and sense of direction. It also helps you to consider your reader, and whether it will be clear to him or her exactly why you make each of the moves you do, and where the whole essay is heading. Similarly, professional philosophical writers are frequently required to produce an abstract of their work, a self-contained summary of its approaches and conclusions. So, even if you started writing with the introduction, it's a good idea to go back and spend some time thinking about it and your conclusion.

Effective communication is what makes good writers stand out. When you are writing essays, it is very easy to fall into the trap of thinking that this is between you and the page and you forget that a real person is going to have to read it and perhaps even enjoy it. Consider your reader.

Unless you are told otherwise, your reader is a well-informed academic who is going to take you and your essay seriously. The style is therefore formal. This does not mean that it has to be long-winded or pompous. It is very often the people who understand their subject best who can explain it most simply and directly. Those who have only half a grasp of what they are talking about are the ones who are most likely to dress up their shallow knowledge in dense language. They think they know what they want to say, but when it comes to putting it down on paper, the words won't come because they have not thought everything through. If you can say what you mean with absolute clarity, you will demonstrate your knowledge effectively. Look at every single sentence you write and ask yourself whether it is crystal clear. Trying to achieve this clarity will often expose a lack of understanding on your part and that is what makes essay writing such a good learning opportunity. You expose the gaps and work on them. Do not be tempted to fudge.

THINGS TO WATCH OUT FOR
The following are the most common *general* problems with the structure and content of philosophy students' essays. If you recognise any of these in your work, take steps to write them out.

- A philosophy essay is not just a list, or a brief history, of different philosophical positions. If you find yourself heading in this direction, you will need to focus: find one or two bits from your list/history that best address the essay question you have been set, and expand your discussion of these. Overall, your essay must be a justified answer to a question.

- No good philosophy essay can come from two (or more) shorter essays that are simply stuck together. This sometimes happens with essay questions that encourage a two- or three-part answer, such as 'Compare X and Y's arguments concerning Z.' Of course, you may write the two or three parts separately, but then they need to be integrated. Even if the essay question has several parts, it is still *one question*.

The task here is to see how one part of your essay leads naturally to, and indeed helps you answer, the next.

- Similarly, when an essay has two or three parts, even if they are successfully integrated they may still be *out of balance*. If, by the time you write to the end of an essay, the word limit threatens and you only have one paragraph to address the third part of the essay question – well, then, you'll need to find a way of downsizing the first two sections. The amount of time, research and the number of words for each sub-topic should reflect its importance to the overall question.

- It is normally insufficient for your essay simply to lay out a philosopher's argument or position. Unless you are clearly told not to, you should always go on to *evaluate* the argument.

- On the other hand, you must not move to the evaluation stage too quickly, especially if you are going to be critical. You have an obligation to give a fair account of any arguments you present. It's too easy to criticise an argument that has been poorly, or too briefly, expressed. Never state an opinion, your own or one that you are trying to criticise, without also expressing as fairly as you can the reasons that are supposed to make it valid.

- One of the most common banes in philosophy essays is a vague use of terminology. Provide at least a provisional definition of key terms early on (perhaps even in the introduction) and then *use those terms consistently throughout your essay*. Of course, your provisional definition may well become more subtle and complex as your essay works through the ideas, and when this happens you should mark it explicitly, perhaps even going so far as to reformulate the definition.

- If after several pages of closely argued philosophical discussion, you conclude by saying something like 'it is all a matter of opinion', then your tutor will hunt you down and berate you soundly.

- In an essay on Descartes, it is completely unnecessary for the introductory paragraph to talk about Descartes' life and times, or even to say 'Descartes was the greatest philosopher of the seventeenth century . . .' Get stuck into the philosophical *problem* and stop wasting time.

A CHECKLIST OF QUESTIONS

Now, take a good break to clear your head. Reread the draft. Ask yourself:

- Have I made it clear what I mean by all the key terms I am using? Have I used them consistently throughout?

- Have I made it clear what each point I make means, and why it is valid? Have I made each point separately and in order, and also made it clear how the points add up logically in order to get somewhere – and ultimately to my conclusion?

- Have I given a more-than-fair and accurate account of all the arguments or positions I discuss? Have I refused the temptation to leave bits out, or exaggerate some things, in order to make an argument look weaker or stronger than it is?

- Imagine that you are someone who doesn't agree with a word you've written. Have you done everything you can to make your points if not convincing at least *plausible* to this most severe critic?

- (By now the essay question ought to be engraved on your heart. But just check again to make sure you have not lost sight of a part of it.) Is every point in the service of answering the question, tied into a clear overall theme, without irrelevancies or 'hot air'? Make absolutely sure that everything you say is relevant. Indeed, you will probably want to *point out why* it is relevant.

- Is the conclusion actually an answer to the set question, and is it clear what my answer is? If you cannot show in your final paragraph that you have answered the question, perhaps you should ask yourself if you really have done so.

- Is every idea my own or, where it is not, has it been clearly referenced back to its source?

Rewrite the draft until you feel you can answer 'yes' to all these questions.

At this point, you will have a good essay. But, it probably still needs some proofreading and preparation for submission. Please see the next section.

There is no one right way to compose a given essay, but there are better and worse ways. Following something like the above procedures should help you to reach one of the better ways.

5.1.4.4 *Proofreading and preparing to submit*

You will no longer fiddle much with the content of your essay. Now, you are concerned with the way that it reads, and the accuracy of the language you have used. *Proofreading is very important.* One of the things your tutors will always look out for, and reward, is tidy, professional, careful work. An essay with misspellings, sentence fragments and such mistakes will be unlikely to get a really good mark.

Proofreading is a skill, and you'll develop it slowly but surely. The first thing to remember is that proofreading is *more* than just 'a quick read through', and *more* than just getting the computer to check your spelling (although that can be helpful).

USING COMPUTER SOFTWARE
Most modern word-processing software packages have pretty sophisticated spelling and grammar checkers. They will not do

all the work for you, to be sure, but they can be a help. Obviously I cannot here tell you how to use these functions, since I do not know what version of software you will be using, but here are some general hints:

- The first thing to do is to make sure that the software knows you want it to check for spelling and grammar. This will involve turning these functions on for the whole of your document, and in particular switching on all the grammar functions. You may also need to tell it what type of English you are using, since the default tends to be American English rather than UK English. Finally, often you can select the level of formality of word usage and grammar: academic essays should be written at, or near, the highest 'formality' level.

- The spelling dictionary will not have many of the technical terms that philosophers use, or many of the names of philosophers. I have had the misfortune to read several essays where the student dutifully followed the computer's advice and corrected 'Descartes' to 'desecrates'! If the computer does not know a word, you can tell the programme to add these to your own personal supplementary dictionary, which you can then store on disk. However, do make sure that, before you add a word, you are actually spelling it correctly.

- The spelling checker will not notice mistypings that result in wrong but correctly spelt words: if you typed 'load' as 'loud', for example.

- Grammar checkers often get obsessed by the length of sentences, and may not be able to distinguish between a long but perfectly acceptable list of things, and an over-complex sentence that needs cutting in half. You'll have to use your judgement.

The most important thing about using a computer in writing, though, is to keep backup copies of your work. You may be allowed to store files on the hard disk drives of the networked computers at university, but that might require you to return to the exact work station. Ask how this works, and also how often these files are cleared. But whether you store your files in this way or not, *also* keep *two* identical copies on two different floppy disks, and keep these disks in different places. Remember, technical problems will almost never be accepted as a legitimate excuse for late or incomplete work.

SHOULD YOU USE FOOTNOTES OR ENDNOTES?
Notes have two purposes. First, under some systems of referencing, the information needed for the reader to find the source of your ideas is put into a note (see section 6.2.1, 'References and bibliographies', below). Second, sometimes you may feel the need to explain or justify a point, or otherwise supply further analysis, but if you did so in the main body of your essay it would just distract the reader from the main purpose of your work. So, you put this further explanation or analysis in a note. In fact, if your essay is properly structured, and if you are strict with yourself about not letting irrelevant points creep into your work, this will rarely happen. The best advice is perhaps not to use notes at all. For referencing, use the Harvard system (see p. 184). For notes that are not references, but are just 'extra' comments on a subject, either include them in the main text if they are important, or cut them out.

However, if you cannot escape using a note, your departmental style sheet may give a ruling on whether footnotes or endnotes are preferred. If not, try to do whatever helps the reader. It is an irritation constantly having to flick to the end of a text. On the other hand, too many footnotes on a page can make for a very ugly appearance. For a few short notes that are important to the understanding of the text, the foot of the page is best. If they are copious and more form than necessity, tuck them away at the end.

PROOFREADING

In your rewrites, and especially in the last ones, proofread for spelling and grammar *without* the help of a computer. Always proofread on a printed-out copy, because it's much easier to miss things when looking at a computer screen. You will need to proofread through the whole text several times because you cannot do all the tasks at once.

First, take a break. It is very difficult to proofread your own work and the more distance you can put between writing and rereading the better. It is obviously a good idea, then, to try to complete an advanced draft very early, so that you can leave it for three or four days. Then, when you pick it up again, you will be unfamiliar enough with what you have written so that awkwardly or unclearly expressed sentences will stand out, along with any remaining typos.

Stage one: Read for general sense and good communication. An excellent suggestion for the last drafts is to read your essay aloud. Strangely, your tongue and lips can often identify unclear sentences and even spelling mistakes much better than your eyes. Are there any bits that are unclear, get your tongue in a twist or sound rather pompous? At this stage, do not stop to correct things or you will lose the big picture. Just make a mark in the margin. Have you got the balance right, spending most time on the most important points? Once you have read right through, wrestle with the awkward sentences. If you are not sure that a long sentence is clear, it's safer to break it up into (grammatically complete) shorter ones. Be careful that any improvements you make do not introduce new errors.
Stage two: Do the mechanical bits in turn. Use the spell checker but do your own check for things that it will miss like *it's/its*, *where/were*. A very common kind of mistake is to mistype the little words, *on* instead of *of* for example. Is your punctuation helpful? Double-check names and dates, physically look up everything that you have cross-referenced. Check your grammar: common errors to look out for include verbs changing tense and pronouns drifting between *one* and *you*, sentences without verbs, run-on sentences where there should

be a full stop in the middle, singular verbs with plural subjects and singular subjects with plural verbs. More about these below.

Stage three: Give it to someone else to read, not necessarily a specialist in your subject. Ask them to make sure they can completely understand every sentence. In this way, they will help you to test your own understanding. (Offer to do the same for them. You can learn a lot about your own writing from helping to make other people's writing clearer.)

Stage four: Check again all your referencing. Is it in the required format (see below)? And have you a reference in the text for every borrowed idea or quotation? Is every text you used (and thus referenced) in your bibliography, and are these entries all in the prescribed format?

Final preparations: There may be a departmental or university style sheet telling you how to set your work out. If so, follow it closely. If not, or if it doesn't cover everything, here are a few suggestions:

1. Make sure your typeface is big enough:
   - Do not use 8 pt type – or smaller – at all, unless you really want to make your tutor grumpy.
   - but 10 pt is just about the limit that older eyes can read comfortably for any length of time. You could use this size of type for footnotes, perhaps.
   - 12 pt is easy on the eye (especially for ageing academics who have a lot of essays to read). 14 pt is also okay.
   - Use only one style of font, and only one font size, throughout the essay. Swapping fonts and sizes looks silly and is confusing. Similarly, use only black ink.
2. Use A4 size paper, of course. Also, a page with plenty of white space is more attractive than a black, solid block of text. Make sure you use generous margins (somewhere over an inch, or around 3cm) so that the marker can write helpful comments. There are two conventions for marking the difference between paragraphs: *either* the first line of each paragraph

should be indented (by a centimetre, say), *or* you should not indent but instead separate paragraphs with a blank line. Do not use both.

3. Attach a cover sheet to your essay, giving the title of your essay, the date submitted, the name of the course and tutor for which it is submitted, and your name (unless you are required to submit anonymously, in which case put your student identification number). On the next page, start the essay at the top of the page.

4. Always use page numbers, and a good idea, too, is to put your name on each page, just in case the staple tears out. If work is submitted anonymously, put your student number on the page instead.

5. The line spacing should be one and a half or, better still, two lines.

6. If you must write by hand (and are allowed to), be as neat as possible, leave generous margins, use only one side of the paper and use black ink.

7. Unless you are told otherwise, don't use plastic folders or spines of any type to bind your essay together. The tutor who marks your work will find them irritating, and there is a real danger that pages will get lost. A simple staple will do.

All the above is summarised in the flow chart (see Figure 5.4).

5.1.4.5 Complete disaster

What do you do if, in spite of all the good advice in this book, you fail to hand your essay in on time? You can no more hand an essay in when you like than you can show up for an examination when you like! However, you may have a good reason, such as illness. Your department will have an 'extenuating circumstances' procedure, and you will have been given information about it, probably in a booklet on the first day at university. If you have been ill, obtain a medical certificate. This procedure will tell you whom to inform, and whom to give the medical certificate to. Similarly, the procedure will tell you whom to inform if you have serious personal problems that interfere with your work. All these are legitimate 'extenuating circumstances', and they may be taken into account if you find you need an extension to deadlines. Having three essays to hand in for the same day does not constitute grounds for an extension. It is merely a fact of university life and a very good reason for organising your time wisely. As soon as you feel you are behind schedule, have a word with your tutor.

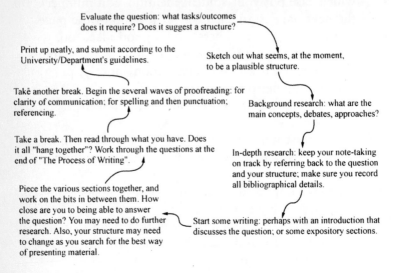

Figure 5.4   The process of writing

If the worst comes to the worst, face up to it. Go to your tutor, lecturer or course organiser, own up and apologise. The longer you leave it, the harder it will be. Do *not* try to explain how your computer ate your essay at the last moment: you should have kept a floppy copy. *Nobody* believes that computers crash two hours before the submission time. By that late hour you should have a copy already printed out for a final proofread. You could hand that copy in if the computer crashes. Better to hand in a late draft than to hand in late. You may find that you will be marked down for late submission but if you have ignored all this advice, that is exactly what you deserve!

The university and/or department will also have regulations

concerning how you can make up work that was not sub-mitted on time, for no good reason. For example, you may be required to write an essay on a new topic over the summer months – and that's no fun at all. You will also likely have your mark automatically reduced (which is only fair, since you will have had longer to work on the essay than your fellow students). The same principles apply to missed exams.

So, you've finished, and handed the essay in. Well then, pat yourself on the back – and start work on the next essay!

5.1.5 The essay returns

Your tutor will now mark your essay, but be patient, it may take a couple of weeks. Find out what the arrangements are for picking up the marked work.

In marking, your tutor will have commented on your essay, both at the end, and along the way, in the margins. These comments are not just the tutor sounding off, but are meant to help you to understand your strengths and weaknesses, and to improve on the latter. So, when you get your essay back, resist the temptation to put it away in a file. Look at the comments carefully. If a few of you can get together and read each other's essays after marking, you will get a much better understanding of what makes a good essay in your subject.

There is no fixed convention for marginal comments. Fre-quently, tutors will just put a tick next to points that they feel have been well made, or a cross next to those that are unclear or unsound. But also, tutors will write out their reasons, such as 'good point!', 'well expressed', 'nice example' – or, on the other hand, 'not clear', 'this doesn't follow', 'how does this relate?', 'explain'. If the comment is positive, to what does it refer, and how does this represent a *general strength of your work*? If the comment is negative, think about what should you have done in that instance, and also think about *what general principle the tutor is employing*, which you could also use to make your next essay better. Since it is important for your learning that you understand both what the comments

mean and what (in future essays) you could do about your
mistakes, don't be the least bit afraid of going to your tutor
and asking: *What does this comment mean?* Or *How can I do
better?*

5.1.6 Finding and using sources

In connection with this topic, you should also read the
'Gathering resources' (see p. 114 above) and section 6.2.1,
on 'References and bibliographies', below.

5.1.6.1 Why use sources?
You need to think, first of all, about why you need to use
primary or secondary sources in your work. A primary source
is a text by a philosopher whose work is part of the topic of
your essay. For example, anything by Descartes will be a
primary source in an essay about Descartes. A secondary
source is a text that is about that topic, but not by the primary
philosopher. So, a book by B. Smith called *Descartes' Theory
of Mind* would be a secondary source.

Well, the reason for using primary sources, then, is clear:
they are the topic of the essay. It would be absurd to write an
essay about Descartes without mentioning any of his work.
Slightly less absurd would be to write about Descartes' philosophy of mind, for example, and mention only *one* of his
works. Especially in a text-based course, and unless you are
specifically told otherwise (e.g. if the set topic were Descartes'
philosophy of mind in the *Meditations*), you should feel
obliged to read the primary sources more widely than you
did in class.

Secondary sources have several roles to play. First, they can
help you come to an understanding of the context of the
primary sources: *why* was Descartes so interested in the mind,
and why did he approach the problem in the way that he did?
Second, they can help you to understand the primary texts
themselves: *how* are we to understand the complex argument
Descartes gives on page 37? We can summarise these first two

roles by saying that secondary texts can help ensure your essay is at least on the right track.

Third, secondary sources can ensure that your way of dealing with a text, problem or issue is sufficiently up-to-date, or at least takes into account up-to-date information. That is, secondary sources are your way of joining and contributing to current debates/theories/evidence in your field. This use of secondary sources is of most significance in advanced under-graduate essays, dissertations and postgraduate work.

Fourth, they can suggest interpretations of Descartes' work as a whole, or of particular issues, that are different from the interpretations you were given in class, or came up with by yourself in the course of reading. That is, secondary sources can help relieve you of a certain narrowness that you didn't even know you had. In such a case, you have several alter-natives: you can abandon your initial interpretation, and go with the one you found in the secondary source; you can decide the secondary text is wrong; or you can find a third interpretation that takes into account both the views. Now we are starting to see the argumentative dialogue that is a feature of most good essays: what you say in your essay should be tested by exposing it to the counter-arguments of others. Only in this way will your work be *balanced*, *reasonable* and *plausible*, rather than *one-sided*.

Balance in your essays is achieved by forcing your own ideas to defend themselves against criticism (sometimes these are criticisms that you *imagine* someone making; more often they will be found in the secondary literature). From this it follows that just because someone has published a paper or a book on Descartes (and thus is an 'authority') does not mean that his ideas about Descartes cannot be challenged. Just like you, the secondary source has to look to the evidence, and has to provide arguments. So, it is by no means impossible that your idea can be defended even where it differs with an authority. (After all, secondary authors disagree with *each other* all the time!) Similarly, even if a secondary author *agrees* with you that isn't worth much unless his or her reasons for agreeing with you are good.

However, there is another side to that coin. When citing a secondary source that is critical of your idea, you must go out of your way to represent these criticisms as *fairly* and *generously* as you can. Otherwise, you will be accused of attacking a 'straw man' – that is to say, an unrepresentatively weak position that is easy to knock down.

The fact that secondary sources can suggest new interpretations also means that they may be written from the point of view of that interpretation. In other words, look out for writers who have certain affiliations with philosophical positions, or who have their own ideas to sell, come what may! Not all philosophers are as 'fair' and 'generous' as we might wish. You need to be as critical about secondary sources as you do about the primary texts.

If you do all this, and your ideas emerge unscathed, then you've written a good essay.

5.1.6.2 *Finding sources*
A word of warning: once you begin a search, you can be overwhelmed with sources of information and you may not yet know enough to be selective. This is why your teachers provide recommended reading lists. Use them.

Your university library will be your best friend. There are two key skills here: first, the ability to use the on-line library catalogue and CD-Rom or Internet-based indexes; second, being able to skilfully browse the shelves.

The library will probably have three technology-based ways of finding sources, and there are two other important resources you can use.

1. The library catalogue, which allows you to search for books in the library.
2. A collection of CD-Rom databases, such as the *Philosopher's Index* (which is also produced in paper form).
3. The library will allow access to Internet-based databases. Ask your librarian.

These last two will be necessary for finding materials published in journals. In addition, there are other Internet databases that can be very useful and that you can use from any Internet connection:

4. Obviously, there are the big general search engines such as Google. The problem with these is that they will probably yield too much information. Other engines, such as Yahoo, have a hierarchically arranged database, which works a bit like the Yellow Pages – this means you find 'philosophy' under Arts and Humanities; and under philosophy, you find 'philosophers', and under that, Descartes. Some indexes are just for philosophy (such as www.personal.monash.edu.au/~dey/phil/). There are even search engines designed entirely for finding philosophical resources (such as hippias.evansville.edu).
5. Finally, you can look at the on-line catalogues of other libraries, or even groups of research libraries, around the world. (Start with copac.ac.uk.) This might enable you to trace a book not in your library that can then be obtained by inter-library loan.

In all of these cases, you need some search skills. You'll probably get furthest with keyword searches. A keyword search employs a compusterised index, and searches for all of the entries in the index that have your keywords within them. There are three steps to such a search.

1. First of all, you need a small collection of keywords based upon the topic you are researching. 'Philosophy' is too broad, but 'Descartes', 'imagination', and 'body' would be better. Using a broad engine like Google, you will need several keywords to narrow down your search usefully, using the library catalogue, probably fewer. Don't forget that UK and US spellings differ: e.g. 'synthesising' versus 'synthesizing'.
2. Then, you will need to enter these keywords into the search engine singly or in combinations. Depending

upon the number and usefulness of the results, add or subtract keywords to narrow or widen the search. You can use 'Boolean' operators to make your search more precise. For example, entering 'Descartes and imagination' would only return records that have *both* those words in it. If you keep getting records that are irrelevant, you can try to exclude them. The usual nomenclature is with a minus sign before the keyword. So: 'Descartes and imagination -mathematics' would exclude entries with mathematics as a keyword. Many engines have an 'advanced search' page that will help you to use Boolean operators and other such subtleties.

3. Finally, you need to filter out what is not useful. Look at the record that returns: what is the title, who wrote it, when, for whom? What other keywords does it contain: do these suggest that the source is heading in your direction? It's probably better to pass over something that would have been useful than to waste your time looking at dozens of books or websites that don't help you at all.

Now that you have the references to various things, you need to find them! Books are on the library shelves, or, if not, look in the short loan or other specialist collection. Journals will be held in their own section of the library, usually alphabetically by title of journal, and then chronologically by the date of the particular number. Books, and articles from periodicals, not held at all by your library can be ordered by inter-library loan. This can take a couple of weeks, and there may be a small fee. Internet sites can be downloaded and/or printed. Internet materials may be articles, but equally likely they will be valuable links to other sites, or references to things in paper form that send you back to your library.

A tutorial in using the Internet for doing research can be found at www.humbul.ac.uk/vts/philosophy/index.htm.

Browsing the shelves is also a great way to find materials. Sometimes, the entry in the library catalogue can be slightly misleading, or even inaccurate. Other students may have found the obvious titles before you (be quicker off the mark next time!), and so you need to look for the less obvious ones. Also, a book may have a chapter on Descartes, but Descartes may not be in the title or one of the keywords. So, an hour spent strolling along the shelves, looking at the tables of contents of books and their indices, can yield rich rewards. Obviously, you will start looking in the most obvious section of the library – with Descartes, for example, in the history of philosophy section. But you'll also need to learn how philosophers divide up their subject (metaphysics, philosophy of science, ethics, etc.). Start with the subject map (Figure 2.1) provided in Part One.

Now, a few practical matters:

- Remember that your research will probably occur in at least three 'waves'. First, some background research, then a wave of more detailed investigation of particular issues or authors, and then (in the middle of writing) perhaps several returns to the sources to chase up ideas that only occurred to you in the act of writing. See the discussion in section 5.1.4, 'The writing process', above.

- Don't over-use sources. You need to show your understanding of primary texts, not just show that you can type them out into your essay! Similarly, secondary sources are there to improve and test your understanding, not substitute themselves for it.

- Make it clear when an idea is yours, and when it is someone else's, and always reference your sources, even when you are not quoting word for word.

- For details about how (and when) to quote, see section 6.2.2.3, 'Using quotations', below (p. 200).

5.1.7 Portfolio of work

A form of assessment that is becoming increasingly common is the 'portfolio'. Clearly, this concept originated within professions such as fine art or architecture. The student or professional would accumulate a body of work that demonstrates his or her mastery of a range of techniques.

So, in a philosophy course, you might be asked to do a number of smaller tasks: book/article reviews or précis, bibliographic searches of materials for some hypothetical essay, brief expositions of philosophical concepts or passages, diagrams or other visual aids, and so forth. A few things to keep in mind:

- Insofar as any piece of work in the portfolio is intended to be anything like a justified answer to a question, then all the above advice on essay writing still applies.

- If as any piece of work in the portfolio is to be written, then all the advice in this part of the book on writing style, referencing, quoting and so forth still applies.

- The purpose of the portfolio is to show your mastery of certain types of knowledge or skill. You may have been given a list of these; if so, tick them off against the pieces in your portfolio.

- You may be asked, as part of the portfolio, to write a self-reflective overview, perhaps meditating on what you have learnt about the subject, and about doing the various types of writing. Spend some time and effort on this part, not only because it is required and marked, but above all because *this type of self-reflection can be very useful to you*. After all, the more you know of your own strengths and weaknesses, the better your assessments for *other* courses are going to be.

- When submitting the portfolio, make sure that nothing is going to fall out of the bundle when it is passed around the department.

5.1.8 The dissertation

Dissertations are frequently required from final-year students, and so will not concern you at all in your first year. However, this book will still be on your shelf in your final year, so a few words about dissertations.

All of the above advice about essay writing still applies, certainly. However, it's important to remember that a dissertation is not *just* a double- or triple-length essay. Why not?

First of all, you pretty much choose you own topic. *This of course is part of the fun*! But choosing a topic that can be accomplished in the time and word limit, and is challenging enough without being beyond your current skills, is tricky. Of course, your supervisor will help you do this, and give you advice on any suggestions you have. Still, choosing your own topic has implications: for example, you will need to do the background research from the ground up, not being able to rely upon a term or semester's course to help prepare you. You'll need to check that your library has sufficient resources for the work, since a course tutor will not have already checked. Also, you will need to justify your choice of topic in the dissertation. While for a course essay, you can safely assume the topic is relevant and interesting (because your tutor set it for you), in the dissertation such assumptions need to be demonstrated.

Second, that last point about justifying the relevance and interest of your topic is part of a larger issue. A dissertation needs to be a complete and self-contained piece of work. With a course essay, you tend to pick up a philosophical 'story' at a certain point (the essay will be on *this* problem in *that* philosopher), and that's acceptable. In the dissertation, you will need to do extra work to 'detach' your topic from out of the larger 'story'. Why is it that you can work on *this* problem/philosopher without also dealing with *that* problem/philosopher? This will test your skills of creatively synthesising materials, and investigating and justifying fundamental claims. Again, this is one key reason why dissertation writing is so rewarding: you get the sense of really tackling a problem, rather than working away at the edges of things.

Third, obviously enough, you are working alone. Certainly, you have a supervisor who will give you advice and read sections. But there are no seminars/tutorials on your topic, and your philosophy mates are off working on *their* dissertations. So, unlike writing essays or revising examinations for a course – where you are permitted and sometimes encouraged to work (up to a point) in groups – writing a dissertation means working solo. The first year at university is difficult because your time is so much less structured than at school/college. The temptation (and each year too many students fall into it!) is to let things slide until it is too late. With your dissertation, your time is *even more* unstructured, and thus relies even more on your time-management and self-motivation skills.

Do make the time spent with your suprvisor count: several days in advance (at least), give to him or her any new drafts of your work to look at, and bring with you all your plans, notes, key texts, and written-down versions of any questions you wanted to ask.

Fourth, even if your dissertation were just like a course essay in the above respects, its length alone would set it apart. Writing a piece of work that is three times longer and more complex, requiring three times the research, note-taking, mind-mapping, draft-writing, and so forth – all this is a *different ball game*. Some students, who are very competent at writing course essays, get buried by the sheer quantity of work for a dissertation, or else produce a piece of work that gushes into several tangents, and lacks an overall direction. Your ability to synthesise materials is again tested, as well as your ability to examine critically your own work. Again, the feeling of real immersion in the subject is a pleasure, and should give you a strong sense of achievement. Obviously, pacing yourself, and staying organised is key. A few good ideas are: (1) map out your time between now and due date, and on this map put things like 'will have read book x by . . .', 'will have written a draft of section x by . . .' and so on. (The date when you plan completion of a full draft of the dissertation should be two weeks before the final deadline. Also, you should aim to have the complete and polished work done two days early (to allow for last-minute disasters).) Then (2) every couple of days, stand back as it were, and take half an hour to review where you've got to and where you're going – hopefully, all this will give you something of the essential sense of control over the material that you need.

The dissertation is a major project; successful completion is a sign that you are ready for anything!

5.2 EXAMINATIONS

Most examination questions will be asking for what boils down to a short essay. So, all the skills we talked about above will apply to examination taking. Of course, there are some very important differences. As obvious as they are, it's still worth thinking about these differences.

- Unlike an essay, you cannot have your research or revision notes with you when you write the answer. This means that memory does play an important role. Put crudely, the exam is testing what you've learnt, not what you've written down in your notes.

- Unlike an essay, you have a very short and precisely pre-scribed space of time for the actual writing. This means that much less emphasis is placed upon composition, style, structure and so forth. The exam is interested in your ability to handle ideas, accurately and concisely, and to think *philosophically* on the hoof.

- Unlike an essay, you do not know the question at the time of doing the background research. This means that the background research and other types of preparation must be wider; examinations test a broader range of material than an essay. Also, it is testing your ability to *apply* your knowledge of the subject to something new and unex-pected.

These three points indicate the purpose of examinations as a type of assessment. Students who are good at exams under-stand what exams expect, and why.

5.2.1 Preparing for exams

Look at past papers. Somewhere in your university there will be kept an archive of past examination papers. Find it and use it: but make sure that neither the course nor the structure of the exam have changed since a past paper.

Read the instructions on the examination paper. How many questions are you going to be asked? How many topics have you covered on the course? How many topics do you need to revise? There may well be some bits of the course that you find easier or more absorbing than others. These are the ones to concentrate on. Just make sure that if you are question spotting, you cover a safe amount of material. It is a good idea to have at least one spare topic in the bank in case one of your chosen subjects does not come up or the question is asked in a way you don't like.

Do the past questions typically ask for certain kinds of philosophical work: for example, definition, critical evalua-tion, contextualisation, compare-and-contrast, or dealing with hypothetical examples?

Here is a sample of an examination paper you might come across in a course on Descartes.

Descartes and Modern Philosophy
First year examination, May 2003

This paper contain SIX questions in TWO parts. You must answer ONE question from EACH part. You have 2 hours.

PART ONE
1. Critically discuss Descartes' argument concerning dreaming.
2. What does Descartes mean by 'thinking'?

---

3. **After Descartes has demonstrated that he exists, what must the next stage of his argument in the *Meditations* be?**

PART TWO

4. **What might Descartes have said in reply to Locke's criticisms of the notion of innate ideas?**
5. **Compare the accounts of imagination given by Descartes and by Hume.**
6. **Compare the accounts of space given by Descartes and Leibniz.**

All the questions are asking you to show your *understanding* of a problem, and then to *employ* that understanding in one or more of the following tasks: evaluation, comparison, contextualisation, or application to a new problem. (For some further advice on how to figure out what questions are asking for, see section 5.1.3, 'First, read the question'.)

Question 1 is a straightforward state-and-evaluate-an-argument type of question. To answer it you'll need to know not only what Descartes' argument actually is, but also what its strengths and weaknesses are, and the reasons why they really are strengths or weaknesses. You could also include some differing interpretations of the argument. But you only have an hour, so don't try to write about *all* of these things!

Question 2 is a definition question. It looks as though you could answer it in a couple of sentences, but that would be unwise. You'd probably also want to look at strengths, weaknesses and implications of Descartes' definition. Why is it important that the 'thinking' is defined in just this way? How does Descartes arrive at the definition?

Question 3 is again looking for you to discuss an argument, but in this case the emphasis is on setting it in *context* – what is the argument trying to achieve, why does Descartes need to achieve this, and how does it follow from previous stages? Contextualisation questions are asking you to employ your understanding of a particular passage in order to arrive at a broader understanding of the whole.

Question 4 is a hypothetical. Since Descartes was dead long before Locke published his essay, Descartes could never have replied. But suppose he could and did, what would he have said? Another type of hypothetical question might be: 'Imagine that Descartes heard "voices" in his head. How would this affect his "I think therefore I am"?' In each case, your task is to put forward analysis or argument that is in the spirit of Descartes. That is to say, an argument that agrees with Descartes' basic principles and methods, but tackles a new problem.

Questions 5 and 6 are comparison-and-contrast questions. The point here is to show that you have a mastery of a topic across two different philosophers. You would be unwise, though, just to write two mini-answers, one on Descartes and one on, say, Hume. Instead, you are looking for important relationships. In other words, for those similarities and differences on this particular problem that tell us something about Descartes and Hume more generally. You probably won't have space to pursue this 'more generally' in your answer, but you should keep it in mind as a way of filtering out similarities and differences that are unimportant.

Plan your revision. You should go over all your selected topics several times. So, instead of planning to do one topic to death before going on to the next, aim to revise all your exam-question topics once and then revise them all again, and again. That way, everything gets a fair turn and nothing gets skimped. It also means that you can get all the library work done in one go, and the rest of your revision can be done just with your accumulated notes.

Revise. Unless you are told otherwise by your tutor, just like an essay you will be expected to have conducted both primary and secondary research on your revision topics. In an exam question on Descartes, your answer should show that you know your way around his writings, and that you are familiar with a handful of interpretations from secondary sources. However, on the exam itself, you will not be expected to come out with quotations, pack your answer with scholarship, or use proper referencing. Instead, it will be sufficient to say something like that 'A. Author interprets Descartes to be claiming that . . .' That is, brief summaries or paraphrases of interpretations, arguments and evidence.

When revising, instead of just reading over your notes, which can put you to sleep or make you think you're learning when you're not, try making notes of your notes, and then notes of *those* notes, until you are down to a postcard's worth or less for each question. Then, check that you can expand it all again to exam-answer size. A glance at these notes before you go into the exam will give you all the confidence you need.

Normally in a philosophy exam, knowing a lot of information is not the main point. But there may be times when having memorised 'six points that can be made on such-and-such an idea' will be helpful. In that case, take a keyword from each of the six, and the first letter of that keyword, then, make up a sentence the words of which have the same first letters.

Do past papers. You might like to brainstorm a few past papers with friends to get ideas on how to structure answers, and, at some point, when you are far enough on with your revision, but well before the examination date, do a paper under exam conditions. That is, get a friend (or perhaps a tutor) to provide you with a question in a sealed envelope, and then sit down with it, a pen, some paper and an alarm clock. If exams are a real weakness, do this several times in consecutive weeks; this should build your confidence no end. You'll also get a sense of how much you can write in the time allowed, and thus how to fit your answers to the time allowed for each question? (See 'Do your sums' below.) If you run out of things to say, you will have to go back to the books. Always revise more than you think you need, of course, to allow for all the things that go straight out of your mind under the stress of the exam.

Another good thing to do with friends on the module is to

brainstorm possible questions – this should help prepare you for different ways in which topics can be worded.

Do your sums. Say the exam starts at 10am. There are two hours and three questions. Plan on 15 minutes to fill in your name, and carefully read and pick questions. That leaves 35 minutes each; but reserve the last five minutes to write your conclusion. When the exam begins, write down your time reminders first:

10.15 Start the first question.
10.40 Write conclusion.
10.50 Start second question.
11.20 Write conclusion.
11.25 Start third question.
12.00 Pen down and smile!

Make sure you know *exactly* where and when the exam is. If you are not a morning person, get an alarm call or ask someone to see that you are up in time. You might be surprised by the number of people who sleep in on an exam morning! It is never a good excuse and will not be treated as one.

5.2.2 On the day

(If you are unable to attend an exam, you must give your reason to the course tutor or departmental office as soon as possible. If the reason is illness, you must produce a medical certificate.)

Get there in plenty of time so that you arrive feeling calm and confident, but do not get there too early; you do not want to hang about with a crowd of hysterical people working themselves into a nervous frenzy. Be sure you have everything you need: identification if required, watch, spare pens and handkerchief. When you go into the examination hall, you will be asked to leave your notes, your coat and your bags at the back of the hall. Be sure to take your purse or your wallet with you.

The best cure for exam nerves is the knowledge that you have studied to the best of your ability. Remind yourself that you are as well prepared as you will ever be and look forward to showing off your knowledge. Your tutors are eager for you to pass and they are actively looking to reward you for displaying relevant understanding. They are not going to try to catch you out. If nerves do begin to get the better of you, before or during the exam, close your eyes and just breathe. Breathe very slowly and deeply, slow-counting to seven as you breathe in. Then see how slowly you can breathe out. Three breaths like this will have you perfectly calm.

Now read the exam instructions: how many questions are there, and are they equally weighted? Does the exam have a structure: do you have to answer one from each of several sections, perhaps? You may be asked to use a fresh examination book for each answer. If so, remember to fill in the cover of each.

If there is anything you need to ask the invigilator, just put your hand up. It does occasionally happen that misprints occur on exam papers, in spite of careful proofreading. If something is missed out from the instructions, or if they are not clear, the invigilator will be glad to hear about it and will inform the rest of the class. If you run out of paper, feel unwell, need to go to the toilet, or need to borrow a pen, put your hand up and the invigilator will come to you. Don't just get up and go to the front or back of the examination room – you can be disqualified for this.

Read through the questions and choose the ones you are going to do. Don't forget that you will be writing brief essays. This means that your choice should not be determined by the fact that you are very familiar with *one part* of a question, because you are going to have to answer the *whole* question. Then, decide on the order in which you are going to do them. Make a note of the time at which you will need to start drawing each question to a conclusion. Make a note of the time at which you stop doing each question, finished or not. Do not be tempted to overrun. Use any time left over to check through your answers, but do not start dithering and changing things that were right in the first place. If in doubt, go with your first instincts. Also, remember that you cannot get less than zero on any one answer, so it is *always worth making an attempt at an answer*. That's why it's important not to overrun the clock on each answer.

5.2.3 After the exam

When the exam is over, avoid people who ask, 'What did you write for question two?' It is over, finished, and there is nothing you can do to change it.

At many universities, it is not normal practice to return exams in the same way as essays are returned. However, and even if you do well, you should still ask if you can make an appointment with your tutor and discuss your result. As with the feedback on your essays, try to look for the general principles behind the good and bad points. Knowing these should help you do even better next time.

Other than simply misunderstanding or misrepresenting a philosophical point, marks are most commonly lost because of:

- Not reading the instructions and doing one question too few or one too many.

- Not reading the question: that is, writing an answer (which in itself might be fine) to the *wrong question*, or just including irrelevant waffle.

- Bad time management, thus leaving yourself too little time for the last question.

5.3 ORAL PRESENTATIONS

Some tutors expect students to give oral presentations in tutorials/seminars, either individually or as part of a small group. It is not very likely that this will happen at the start of your first year. By the time you have to give a talk, it will be mid-year and you will be familiar with your subject and friendly with the other members of the tutorial group, who are all going to have to go through the same torment.

Sometimes these presentations will not be directly assessed. That is, they will not be marked and the mark carried over into your final grade for the course. But, on other occasions, they will be marked just as if the presentation were an essay.

You will find the outline of a sample presentation in Part One of this book, see page 46 above.

5.3.1 Preparing and presenting

Your oral presentation will be based on a paper (or, at least, detailed notes and structure for a paper) that you have written in advance, and this should be produced with all the skills you would use for writing an essay. However, few tutors will be happy if you simply read from your written paper, and your fellow students will be bored to tears. Nothing is worse than someone mumbling out a paper, head buried in their notes! So, as part of your preparation for the presentation, keep the following in mind:

- Your presentation will be very similar to an essay in structure and content. But remember that a *reader* can always go back and read a bit again; *a listener* cannot. Therefore, in your presentation you will probably need more explanation on each point, and extra examples or analogies. In short, you will be able to 'do' less in the same number of words.

- Practise more than once in front of a mirror, or a friend. Work on eye contact and keep a easy, steady pace throughout.

- You may have been given lower and upper time limits for your presentation. Time yourself in practice. The odds are that you will speed up your delivery on the day, so don't worry too much if you are edging towards an upper time limit. A good speaking pace is between 120 and 140 words per minute. Anything above 150, and you'll need to find a way to make yourself slow down. One technique is to focus on breathing: if you are nervous and are reading too fast, your intakes of breath will automatically become quick, sharp gasps. The tendency is to run out of air before the end of a sentence, and thus speed up even more to compensate. Make your breathing more relaxed and full, however, and your delivery pace will slow too.

- If you feel you are likely just to read from the paper, force the issue: don't write everything out in prose, instead, just bring in detailed notes. Perhaps use 'cue cards': a small pile of postcards, each with a new stage of the presentation summarised on it.

- With your tutor's permission, plan to make use of any appropriate audio-visual aids (whiteboard, overhead projector, PowerPoint slides, recordings). If the structure of your presentation has more than three key points, or if you are working through a complex argument or lengthy quotation, then some kind of visual aid is in order. Don't forget that you may need to organise the equipment and print up, for example, acetates in advance. It may be that a photocopied handout is the best, and simplest, approach.

  On OHP or Powerpoint slides a font size of around 24 will work nicely, but in a big room you'll need a larger font, and it will vary with the projector's resolution, so if possible try things out in advance. Finally, be sparing with the amount of information you put on each slide. You don't want your audience so busy reading a slide that they aren't listening to what you say!

And then, in the presentation itself:

- Try to keep your voice interested and interesting; make sure your voice projects to those sitting furthest away from you; and listen to the speed with which you are speaking and try not to rush.

- Don't bury your nose in your paper; as you speak, make eye contact with your fellow students and the tutor.

- Smile; try to look as though you are enjoying yourself at least a little, and that you have enthusiasm for the subject;

- If you are giving your presentation standing, beware of pacing, shuffling, or rocking from side-to-side (it happens!). If you must move, try to make the movements correspond to new points in the paper.

- Invite questions and comments and be prepared to deal with them. Indeed, don't just say at the end 'any questions?' Instead, be proactive and at a couple of points in your presentations say something like 'this point is quite difficult; perhaps we should talk about it after I'm finished.' Suggested questions or topics for debate can be put in your handout or visual aid.

5.3.2 Working in groups

You may be required to prepare and present a presentation in groups, anywhere from two people on up. All of the above advice still applies. However, some new issues arise.

- When working on a group presentation, it is everyone's responsibility to work at preparation and delivery. The way that groups work, though, ensures that someone is bound to want to boss the rest of you around. This can be very annoying, but it can also be useful, to keep things moving along. A bossy person who has a modicum of responsibility, and is not too domineering, is to be welcomed. Of course, two different people may want to boss everyone around. The way to make this work is to formalise roles, which is always a good idea anyway in teamwork. Each member of the group is the 'boss' of a team working on a certain aspect of the project (doing this bit of background research, for example, or writing out a particular passage). Everyone belongs to more than one team; that way, everyone gets to be boss and bossed equally. The job of these bosses is to ensure their aspect is completed on time and, in order to do this, to delegate responsibility for smaller jobs.

- If group meetings drag on without decisions being made, encourage the group to set itself deadlines 'This meeting will be finished by 3 p.m., and by that time we will have decided . . .'

- Make sure everyone has a contact number for everyone else (or email, provided everyone in the group really does check their email every day). Someone will probably need to keep ringing people to make sure they know what their job is and when it needs doing by. This person can be named the 'executive secretary' of the group, if you must. That some-one may be you: be prepared to take up the reins gladly! If you do so, however, try to avoid becoming a nuisance to your fellow group members by ringing too often or by adopting an officious tone.

- Almost inevitably, there will be one or two people who will try not to do their share of the work. The best way to get them to do their share is, at meetings of the group, and starting with the first meeting, to make it as clear as possible who is doing what task, and by when. That is, A's job is to read and make notes on these two articles by Thursday next week; B's job is to do background research on a particular philosopher or problem by the same date, and so on. Your tutor may be able to offer further advice on dealing with particularly unco-operative students!

• The group should meet several times in advance of the presentation. Make sure the group knows the time and place of the next meeting; also make sure that arrangements are made such that members of the group can communicate difficulties to the others. (For example, a note on a particular noticeboard in the department.)

• The presentation too will be divided up into aspects or parts. It's a good idea, though, to have only one person (or a sub-group headed by one person) prepare the visual aides – so that they are all done in the same style and to the same quality.

• Each member of the group should have a roughly equal role in the delivery. X does the introduction; Y does the first topic; and so on. Normally, the student speaking the words has written them too. But you should always agree in advance that it's acceptable to make critical comments on each other's sections. Only in this way can you achieve a consistency of style of writing, style of delivery, pitch (that is, the level of difficulty or sophistication of the writing) and, above all, *consistency of message*. Also, of course, the whole will need to fit inside a time limit. The group may need to decide who has to make cuts. Don't be tempted to just speak faster.

• To achieve all this, it's important that the group practises as a whole, and runs through the whole presentation *more than once* before the event itself. The aim is to make each section as good, and as integrated with the rest, as possible. Also, you will want to get the transitions between sections to run smoothly.

• Get one person, perhaps the student speaking last, to be the 'coxswain'. Everyone who speaks knows to look at this person every once in a while, and to look for two particular hand gestures. One to indicate 'slow down', the other to indicate 'speak up'. As any time you speak, nervousness can make you race through the words; also, it is very difficult to tell if your voice is carrying adequately. Both these things are crucially important for a successful presentation.

6 GENERAL SKILLS HANDBOOK

6.1 ARGUMENT AND JUSTIFICATION

An essay (or an oral presentation, or an examination answer) is the construction of a justified answer to a question. We've talked a lot above about the 'construction' part – about how to put an essay together so that it is clear, well organised and well resourced. But what about the 'justified' part?

This section will contain some basic advice about employing informal deductive arguments. The next section will speak about arguments particularly based upon examples or analogies.

But we are no longer just talking about *your* essays and *your* arguments. The comments in the following sections should help you in your reading of other philosophers' work. In reading, you must constantly be asking: 'Is this argument valid? Why or why not?', 'What assumptions are being made, and are they good ones?' and 'Does this example/analogy work, or is it misleading?'

6.1.1 Critical thinking

6.1.1.1 *What is an argument?*
In philosophy, by 'argument' we mean 'something which attempts to prove, starting from premises, the truth of a conclusion'. Let us define the terms set out in the above definition.

'*To Prove*' means to *compel belief rationally*. If something is proved, then I have no choice, as a reasonable person, but to believe it. Otherwise, I am not rational. For our purposes, '*rationally*' here means '*logical*'. It does not mean to persuade by violence, trickery, bribery, rhetoric, emotion and so on.

Thus, if I use rhetorical tricks of language to persuade my reader (for example, if I use flowery or showy language to make something sound good) then this is not proof. Again, if I merely appeal to the emotions of my reader, then this too is not proof; for example, describing the pain and suffering inflicted upon one group of people by the act of another may elicit sympathy, but does not necessarily mean that the act was morally wrong.

The first important distinctions we need to make are between premises, the conclusion, and any intermediate steps between them.

The *premises* are any statements that we have to make which are not themselves proven at the moment. (At the moment – they may in fact be the conclusions of previous arguments!) Premises may be incontrovertible pieces of knowledge, or they may be hypotheses that we make 'for the sake of argument . . .' For the argument to be considered successful, all these premises must be (although they may not be initially) clearly stated. No verbal trickery; no rhetorical persuasion; no appeals to that which is outside of reason.

The *conclusion* is whatever proposition the argument is attempting to prove overall. The aim is for the argument to be structured such that if the premises are true, there is no rational choice but to accept the conclusion.

Intermediate steps are the various stages of preliminary conclusions that we reach on the way to the real conclusion. Each step is the conclusion to a previous mini argument, and each step is a premise for the next mini-argument.

6.1.1.2 What kinds of argument are there?
Two other sections of this book are relevant here. First, section 5.1.5 above on 'Finding and using sources', which has some important comments on arguments from *authority*. Second, the section 6.1.2 below on 'Examples and Analogies'.

DEDUCTIVE ARGUMENTS
These are arguments that proceed without any room for probability. For example,

- X is a book.

- All books have pages in them.

- Therefore, X has pages in it.

The conclusion follows from the earlier steps in such a way that *if* the earlier steps are true, it is impossible for the conclusion not to be true. In other words, the conclusion *follows necessarily* from the premises. It is often said that the premises 'imply' the conclusion, but that is a *misuse of the word 'imply'*, which means something quite different (to indirectly suggest). Instead, philosophers say that the premises 'entail' the conclusion.

Such an argument always claims, then: premises *plus* reasoning *entail that* the conclusion is true. There are actually very few different *forms* of reasoning (the inner structure of the argument); the study of these is logic. However, while there may only be a few forms, the *content* of arguments (what the arguments are about) can vary infinitely. Logic (or, more generally, critical reasoning) is powerful because the very few forms cover such a vast number of possible real arguments.

INDUCTIVE ARGUMENTS
You may have noticed that in the example of deduction above, we said that there is no room for probability, and, yet, clearly the premises are only probable. How *certain* am I that all books, without any exception, have pages in them? So, frequently, the premises of *deductive* arguments will be *inductive*. What does this mean?

On the basis of a series of observations of something, I make a generalisation about it. For example, having observed student behaviour for years, I conclude that student gatherings during the daytime are most likely to be because they have a lecture. The conclusion is obviously only probable. There may be many other reasons for the gathering (Union meeting, protest, free lunch, etc.). Inductive arguments move from observations to probable generalisations. They are the kinds of arguments that, in much more sophisticated forms, are characteristic of a key part of scientific enquiry. Suppose I make a series of observations about patients' blood pressure after their taking a certain drug. I can then make an inductive claim about the effect *in general* that this drug has on blood pressure. Further, without this generalisation, the observations are of little use. Such arguments are much less frequent in philosophy essays (cf. the discussion of 'examples' below).

The conclusion to the inductive argument can be used as a premise in a deductive argument. For example:

> Student gatherings during the daytime are *most likely* to be because they have a lecture.
> Students are gathering in room 28.
> Therefore, it is *most likely* that a lecture is about to be held in room 28.

Notice that the *structure* of the argument is still deductive, still purely logical. However, the important part of the argument consists in arriving at the empirical premise, the truth of which is only a probability. *Statistics* is the mathematical tool that evaluates the level of probability of such statements. The 'most likely' of the premise is passed to the conclusion, even though the logic of the argument has nothing merely probable about it.

6.1.1.3 A more careful look at premises

The premises are the starting points of an argument. They are assertions we must assume to be true in order for the argument to get off the ground.

Some premises are *definitions*; others are *factual assertions* about things. 'X is a book' is a factual assertion about a thing. It is contingent whether it is true or false: that is to say, it just happens to be the case that X is a book, and not a kumquat. Some factual assertions are pretty straightforward (such as 'X is a book'); others are more obviously *inductive* in character ('the majority of children are not allergic to peanuts').

'All books have pages' seems to be a definition, or rather the relevant part of a definition, of a thing (namely a book). A definition explains what a thing is. It cannot be otherwise than its definition, and still be what it is. That is, a book without pages just isn't a book. This 'cannot be otherwise' is the mark of a definition. But suppose someone notices a book without pages, like an encyclopedia on a CD-Rom. Then our definition turns out to have been a factual assertion in disguise. In other words, some apparent definitions rely upon factual assertions. Be careful!

When you are reading a philosophy text, remember that some premises may come from other arguments, before or after. In other words, a long passage of philosophy may be like a chain. Each link in the chain is a simple argument, the conclusion of which forms the premise for the next link. Analyse the smaller, simpler links first, before attempting to analyse the whole.

Also, of course, the philosopher may not have written his or her argument in the order that you feel is most logical. He or she may have put the conclusion first, and some of the premises last, for example. You may need to chop and change a passage considerably in order to put it into its logical order.

Finally, while you are reading and thinking about arguments, you may find that an argument needs (in order to be valid) a premise that the author does not supply. Let us call such a premise an *assumption*. This does not necessarily invalidate the argument, of course, it just means that you are being more careful than the philosopher you are reading. Well done!

6.1.1.4 *Validity and soundness*
Validity means that the logical form or structure of the argument is just fine. In other words, *if* all the premises are true, *then* the conclusion must be. However, saying an argument is valid says nothing, yet, about whether the premises are in fact true; nor does it yet say whether we must, in fact, accept the conclusion.

Soundness means both that the logical structure of the

argument is valid, *and* that the premises are all true. It must follow that the conclusion is also true.

The following argument is perfectly valid, but still unsound:

- Stoke-on-Trent is a town in France.

- No towns in France are inhabited entirely by vampires.

- Therefore, Stoke-on-Trent is not inhabited entirely by vampires.

It is valid because *if* the premises were true, *then* the conclusion *must* follow. It is unsound because the premises are not all true. Note that, in this example the conclusion is true, as a matter of fact. But its truth is not justified by a sound argument that precedes it. So, the logical validity of an argument is independent from the truth of either the premises or the conclusion. Unsound arguments can have true conclusions; invalid arguments can have true premises and even true conclusions!

From all we have said, it follows that *all arguments will have the following basic structure*, although some will be much simpler, and others much more complex:

- (Assumption 1)

- (Assumption 2, etc.)

- Premise 1

- Premise 2, etc.

On the basis of assumptions and premises:

- Intermediate Step 1 (following from some combination of the assumptions and premises)

- Intermediate Step 2 (following from some combination of the assumptions, premises, *and previous steps*)

- Intermediate Step 3, etc.

On the basis of assumptions, premises and intermediate steps:

- Conclusion

6.1.1.5 *The basic logical rules of valid arguments*

On your university degree, you will probably take at least one course in formal logic. In that course, you will be taught a sophisticated artificial language for describing logical relationships. You will be expected to take this to heart, and use it where appropriate on other courses. So, the following brief discussion will probably be quickly surpassed. However, even in philosophy papers, not *all* arguments are presented in the artificial language, and certainly not in more 'ordinary' circumstances. So, perhaps, there is also a role for a much more informal way of talking about logical relationships.

For the most part, well-educated human beings have a pretty good sense of what makes a decent argument, even without logical training. Here, we're going to rely upon that. Instead of providing an exhaustive set of rules for valid arguments, we're only going to provide a few. However, we will then also provide a few of the most common (and most commonly *overlooked*) invalid forms. Together, these should set you on the right path to successfully analysing and building arguments.

BASIC ARGUMENT FORMS
Consider the following:

> *If Maurice comes in wearing his hat, then it must be raining.*
> *Maurice is wearing his hat, therefore it must be raining.*

Now, of course, we could question the premises: there may be other reasons why Maurice is wearing his hat. But, for the moment, our job is not to ask whether the premises are true, but instead to ask, 'What is entailed *if* the premises are true?' To discuss this, we need to ignore what the premises are *about* (Maurice, hats, rain). The most important, and the first, lesson of logic is to abstract from the content of statements (what they are about) and focus on their form. (The same is true of algebra; you manipulate algebraic expressions in the abstract, having no idea what numbers x or y stand for.)

Suppose we let A equal 'Maurice is wearing his hat', and B equal 'It is raining.' Then the argument looks like:

If A is true, then B is true.
A is true.
Therefore, B is true.

We have successfully abstracted from the content of the argument, and found its fundamental form. Assigning the letters 'A' and 'B' helped us to do this, and it also helped us to clarify exactly what were the premises and conclusions. The above is probably the most common basic form of valid argument. It has a Latin name: *modus ponens* ('mood that affirms'). To make it even simpler, let's leave out the 'is true', leaving our first valid argument form:

1. If A then B
   A
   Therefore, B.

Here and throughout the following, 'A' or 'B' stand for simple statements (such as 'Headless horsemen exist' or 'Werewolves come out on full moons'). Such statements must either be true or false.

These statements can be modified or conjoined in various ways:

• 'Not A' means 'It is false that A'.

- 'A and B' means the compound statement that 'A and B are both true'.

- 'A or B' means the compound statement that 'either A, or B, or both, are true';

- Where there are compounds in parentheses, this indicates that the compound is to be considered first, before any other compound. So, the expression 'Not (A and B)' means that it is the whole compound 'A and B' that is being negated.

- Finally, 'If A then B' means that, well, 'if A is true, then B will also be true'.

So, let's have a look at a few of the more common argument forms. (Again, this is not a complete list.) Each is followed by a deliberately silly example. Spend some time thinking about each example, till you see how it embodies the rule.

2. Not (A and B)
   Therefore, not A or not B
   It is false that there are both headed and headless horsemen. Therefore, there are either no headed, or there are no headless, horsemen.
3. Not (A or B)
   Therefore, Not A and Not B
   It is not the case that 'Either Jack the Ripper killed only men, or he killed only young women'. Therefore, Jack the Ripper did not kill only men, and he did not kill only young women.
4. A or B
   Not A
   Therefore, B
   At least one of the following is true: 'the house is haunted' or 'someone is playing a trick on us'. But it is false that the house is haunted. Therefore someone is playing a trick on us.

5. A or B (but not both: this is called an 'exclusive or', sometimes written 'xor')
A
Therefore, not B.
> At least one of the following is true, but not both: 'the house is haunted' or 'someone is playing a trick on us'. The house is haunted. Therefore no one is playing a trick on us.

6. If A then B
Not B
Therefore, not A
> If it is dawn, the vampires will be back in their coffins. The vampires are not back in their coffins. Therefore, it is not dawn.

This argument also has a Latin name: *modus tollens* ('mood that denies').

Importantly, this argument is the basic form of the argument type called *reductio ad absurdum* ('Reduction to absurdity'). In this argument, we prove a conclusion (here, not A) by first assuming its opposite (A). Then, we prove that the opposite cannot be true because it leads to a false (or self-contradictory and thus absurd) conclusion. Our conclusion must follow. For example:
> Suppose you really did see a vampire at noon yesterday. (V)
> Then that would mean a vampire was not in its coffin during the day. (If V then not C)
> But vampires are always in their coffins during the day. (C)
> Therefore, you didn't really see a vampire at noon yesterday. (not V)

7. If A then B
If B then C
Therefore, if A then C.
> If there is fog, then there is evil. If there is evil, then the devil's around. Therefore, if there is fog, then the devil's around.

8. If A then B
   If B then A
   If and only if A then B
   > *If there is fog, then there is evil; AND if there is evil, then there is fog. Therefore if and only if there is fog, then there is evil.*

   Note that 'if and only if' is sometimes written as 'Iff'.
9. If A then B
   If C then D
   A or C
   Therefore, B or D
   > *If we go left, we go into the haunted forest. If we go right, we go into the sorcerer's evil realm. We must go left or right. Therefore, we're either going into the haunted forest, or we're going into the sorcerer's evil realm.*

   Notice that B and D could in fact be the same, in which case we're in a classic *double bind*. Damned if we do, damned if we don't!

USING THESE ARGUMENTS

We can use these basic arguments to analyse arguments, or to construct new arguments. Especially when you are analysing existing arguments (perhaps an argument that you found in Descartes), the first step is always to identify what the conclusion is supposed to be, and what premises are being put forward. Then, you should translate it into its logical form. Perhaps with some help from the above argument forms, the validity of the argument should then be apparent. (Although remember that the above is not a complete list.)

Suppose you came across the following passage:

> *The 'argument from design' aims to prove God's existence from the nature of things in His creation. It begins by observing that objects that are made according to a plan always show a trace of that plan. Correspondingly it observes that things that are not made according to a plan show no such traces; or if they do, then it can always*

be shown that the apparent trace is an illusion. The argument continues by asserting that there are many, perhaps all, things in nature that show the trace of being made according to a plan. From that it follows that there must be a creating God.

The conclusion that this argument is trying to reach is that God exists. We'll abbreviate this as statement G. The following seem to be key premises:

- If something is made, then it will show a trace. (If M, then T)

- If something is not made, then it will not show a trace. (If not M, then not T)

- Many things in nature show the trace. (T)

The second and third premises form the *modus tollens* (see point 6 above). We can therefore conclude M (which we can express something like 'Many natural things are made'). It turns out that the first premise above wasn't even necessary!

So we have M. But how do we get to the conclusion G? There seem to be two missing premises needed (we have agreed above to call such missing premises 'assumptions'):

- If natural things turn out to have been made, then there must be a creator. (If M then C)

- God is defined as the creator (G = C).

We easily reach the intended conclusion (G). The argument appears to be valid. Whether it is sound or not is a different matter.

Notice that few of these premises can be lifted, word for word, from out of the text. For example, in the above we assumed that 'made according to a plan' is not really adding anything to just 'made'. We also left out the bit about apparent traces in unmade things being an illusion that can always be unmasked. In other words, *we have to interpret the text's meaning*, as carefully as possible, in order that we can then state the premises in a manner sufficiently clear and simple. This process of interpretation is a key skill in philosophy; much of your essay writing is designed to give you practice. It also follows that, in many real examples of arguments from philosophy texts, there will be a real question of how the argument should be analysed. That's one reason why there is not just one book on Hume or Kant, but dozens on each. This does not mean that just *any* interpretation goes, though!

Let's try another:

> *Let us suppose that there are two things, x and y, and that x is the cause of y. In order for x to be the cause of y, x at some point must have had an effect on something. We'll call this intermediate effect, x_2. (Intermediate because it is not yet y.) Presumably, x_2 then brings about y. But that would mean that x causes x_2, and that x_2 causes y. Again, that means that x must have had an effect on something intermediate, we'll call that x_3; and x_2 must have had an effect on something, and we'll call that x_4. And so on, ad infinitum. What is becoming clear is that at no point can the cause of a thing, or the 'effect' either, for that matter, be identified – you could never point to it, it is always somewhere else. Therefore, we cannot suppose that x is the 'cause' of y. Such a claim is absurd. Our normal concept of a cause is quite meaningless.*

This is a rather complex argument, though not necessarily a good one. It is probably best to split the argument into two, one enveloping the other. The conclusion to the most enveloping argument is that 'The concept of cause is meaningless' (I).

The enveloping argument is relatively simple – except that its first premise is missing. The argument looks like:

- If the concept of a cause is meaningful, then the concept should be able to identify (point to) the cause. (If not I, then P)

- The concept cannot identify or point to the cause. (not P)

- Therefore, the concept of a cause is meaningless. (I, by *modus tollens*)

The conclusion to the second argument is something like: 'The concept of a cause cannot identify or point to the cause' (not P) which was the key premise in the first argument. The argument looks like this:

- To identify or point to the cause means to be able to single out the cause. (P = S)

- Suppose there to be a cause. (C)

- If there is a cause, then there must be an intermediate effect. (If C then N)

- Any such intermediate effect would be a second cause. (N = C2)

- Therefore, there is a second cause. (C2)

- If there is both a cause and a second cause, then the cause is not 'singled out'. (If (C and C2) then not S)

- Therefore, the cause is not singled out. (not S)

- Therefore, the concept of a cause cannot identify the cause. (not P)

This is one way, at least, of interpreting the above argument. Few if any of the steps, or their logical interrelation, could be lifted word-for-word from the text. In order to think the reasoning through, we introduced the concept of 'singling out', which seems a plausible way of understanding what the author meant by 'identify' or 'point to'. This also means that the infinite series of intermediate causes and effects, which the original argument used to such a dramatic effect, is not really necessary. There only need to be two places where one can locate the cause for 'not singled out' to be true. But is this the only way, and the best way, of interpreting the argument?

Notice that there is something slightly peculiar about the argument: we claimed that there was a cause in order to prove that the concept of a cause was flawed! What is happening is that the argument is proposing a hypothesis (C) that, presumably, its opponents would agree with – and then deducing from that hypothesis a conclusion that those same opponents would not agree with. This is a cousin of the *reductio ad absurdum* discussed above.

The conclusion to the enveloped argument then forms an important premise in the enveloping argument. We should point out again that the formal validity of the argument does not prove that it is sound.

A NOTE ON REAL ARGUMENTS
In the examples above, it was pretty clear where the argument begins and ends. But even here, in the first example, we had a premise that turned out to be superfluous. When looking at 'real world' arguments (from books, newspapers, etc.) you will find a simple argument can be buried. There are two possibilities: either it will be mixed up with a previous argument that is justifying one of its premises (or perhaps an argument that uses the conclusion and carries on to some further conclusion). In other words, there may be (even in a relatively brief paragraph) several mini-arguments that culminate in a conclusion. Or, sometimes there is just stuff that doesn't matter. That is, there may be sentences that are just window dressing. So, in looking at real arguments, part of the task is to isolate those statements that form part of an argument, and trying to ignore the rest. Both of these possibilities show why it's important to look for the conclusion first – since working backwards from that point can often help weed out what is inessential.

6.1.1.6 Some of the most common fallacies
Some of the following are logical fallacies: that is, they involve

an error in logic. Even if the premises are true, then the argument must be rejected. Others are just types of bad arguments that are sometimes presented as if they are good arguments.

1. 'SOME' DOES NOT ENTAIL EITHER 'ALL', OR 'THIS ONE'
The Illustrated History of Witches *is a book. Some books have pictures.*
Therefore, The Illustrated History of Witches *has pictures.*

Don't be confused by the book being entitled 'Illustrated', don't even be confused if the conclusion is, in fact, true. This argument is invalid.

2. IF A THEN B, THEN IT IS NOT THE CASE THAT IF NOT A THEN NOT B
The basic reason is that there may be other reasons for the truth of B. For example:

If the town is French then it is haunted by ghosts.
Stoke-on-Trent is not a town in France.
Therefore, Stoke-on-Trent is not haunted by ghosts.

This is clearly invalid!

3. IF A THEN B DOES NOT ENTAIL IF B THEN A
For example:

If something is a werewolf, then it is brown. Fido is brown.
Therefore, Fido is a werewolf.

(BUT: *If* and only if *it is a full moon, then the werewolves will be out.*
The werewolves are out. Therefore, it is a full moon. This is a *valid* argument, because 'if and only if' is a different logical operator.)

4. NOT (IF A THEN B) DOES NOT ENTAIL IF A THEN NOT B
*It is false that 'if something is a ghost, then it is evil';
therefore, if it is a ghost, then it is not evil.*

It could be that *some* ghosts are evil!

5. BEGGING THE QUESTION
Begging the question can be one of the most difficult logical
errors to spot. In this error, an argument assumes as a premise
precisely what it is setting out to prove. Not surprisingly, when
you assume what you are trying to prove, the proof becomes
very easy, and also fairly meaningless!
Let's start with an easy one:

Mr. X is an honest man – he told us so himself!

Consider the following example:

a. If something at X comes from Y, then Y must be a
   different place to X.
b. I have ideas;
c. Ideas must come from somewhere.
d. The ideas must come from a different place to my
   mind.
e. Therefore, ideas must come from outside my mind (i.e.
   from the world).

This argument may look plausible, but it is deeply flawed.
There are several ways to interpret the flaw; one is 'begging the
question'. The aim is to prove that there is some other place
than my mind – that my mind is not in a space all its own, but
is located in a space filled with other objects. But that there are
at least two 'places' is already *assumed* in the opening premise
– that is, 'come from somewhere' is interpreted *spatially*. The
main content of the conclusion is assumed in the premise.
('Come from somewhere' could be interpreted *temporally* –
one idea generates the next, or, as in the philosopher Berkeley,
theologically: all my ideas come from God.)

We should note that there is always a sense, in perfectly valid logical arguments, in which the conclusion is 'contained within' the premises. The premises, as it were, unfold their *combined* logical content to reveal the conclusion. Begging the question is something more than this: first of all, the conclusion is effectively contained in just *one* of the premises; and, second, the conclusion is not 'folded up' in the premise, but is there as itself.

6. ARGUMENT FROM AUTHORITY

An argument from authority is when we claim that something is true because so-and-so says it is, and is an expert in the subject. Now, such an argument *can* provide perfectly good evidence for the truth of a claim. It all depends on the independent verification of the expertise of the authority. Otherwise, arguments based on authority frequently fall into the begging the question trap. If we are reasoning in the following way, we're in trouble: 'The authority is correct about A because she is an authority, and she is an authority because she is correct about A.'

Another problem with authority arguments concerns the relevance of the authority. A specialist in brain surgery is an authority, but you wouldn't ask him or her for an authoritative comment on the likely winner of next year's Wimbledon, would you?

7. HIDDEN CONTRADICTION

Arguments sometimes end up contradicting themselves, often in subtle ways. Consider:

For any adequate explanation of our sensations in terms of a source outside of us, there will be at least one other such explanation that is also adequate.

Therefore, no explanation about an external source for our sensations is invulnerable to doubt.

Therefore, we cannot know that there exists any outside source at all for our sensations.

Descartes is sometimes thought about in these terms. But this is a bad argument: for, the first premise assumes that there are *only* adequate explanations of sensations in terms of a source outside of us, but the conclusion, in order to be true, has to assume some *other* type of explanation as an alternative. (The argument should conclude: 'We cannot be certain *which* outside source is the real source.')

8. A FALSE EQUATION
   That bridge is sound; sounds are vibrations in the air; therefore, that bridge is a vibration in the air.

This clearly assumes that two quite different meanings of the word 'sound' are the same. (Immanuel Kant's critique of Descartes' famous 'I think, therefore I am' has a similar structure. Kant claims that the first 'I' in the statement means something different (and something less) than the second 'I'.)

9. DEFINITION/EXISTENCE ERROR
For example:

   All ghouls are the living dead; therefore, there exist some living dead things.

Just because something can be defined, discussed, debated about, studied – doesn't mean it actually exists. It's probably worth pointing out, however, that just because something doesn't actually exist doesn't mean it cannot be important, influential and so on. For example, the goddess Athena.

10. AD HOMINEM ARGUMENT
Suppose someone X comes up with argument A. If I counter argument A by attacking X ('Mr X cannot be trusted, look at his record!'), then I am arguing 'against the person'. Such arguments are all too common in amateur debating – and all too common also in professional but unscrupulous debating. Who X is, their character, background and even credentials are all irrelevant to the soundness of A. The only exception

would be if X's beliefs, experiences or authority are used as a premise of A. Then, and only then, would an *ad hominem* argument be permissible.

11. ARGUMENT BY SELECTIVE EVIDENCE OR EXAMPLE
The premises of your arguments can be backed up by evidence and by examples. But these must be chosen so as to represent accurately the whole field of possible evidence and examples. For example, suppose I tried to argue that all dogs are black by pointing to a single black dog. That would just be silly. See section 6.1.2, on 'Examples and Analogies', below.

12. MISREPRESENTING THE NATURE OF A DISTINCTION
Sometimes we are tempted to simplify things by claiming that something must be either A or Z, when in fact it could be something in between. For example, an argument might rely on a distinction between good and evil. The possibility of something being neither of these, or in between them, might wreak havoc on the argument.

There is a similar issue when dealing with complex problems and solutions. For example, suppose someone argues that a certain reform of the law would lead to more just convictions in the courts. Suppose then that I counter-argued 'But that wouldn't solve the *whole* problem of justice, would it?' Well, my objection might be true, but is not really a counter-argument. Maybe only a dozen different *simultaneous* reforms would solve the *whole* problem, but any one of them might still be a good idea on its own.

Finally, sometimes we are tempted to claim that because A and Z belong to a continuous scale, there is no real difference between A and Z. This is sometimes called a 'sliding scale' argument. Just because there is no definite age at which a young person becomes an old person doesn't mean that there are no young and no old people.

13. SLIPPERY SLOPE
This is often used in morally or politically loaded arguments. For example, a common objection to the legalisation of

cannabis is that it is just one perilous step closer to our falling into a society that permits the usage of cocaine or heroin. The assumption here is that one step down a road will make it more difficult, or impossible, not to take the next step. Well, in some cases, this assumption may be true as a matter of fact, but it cannot be *assumed* true in all cases.

6.1.1.7 Evaluating the premises

So far, we have only discussed validity: whether or not the logical form of an argument is fine. But the *soundness* of an argument requires more than this. It also requires *true premises*. So, how do we go about evaluating the premises?

1. Well, in part, we look for the arguments that justify those premises. In other words, we repeat the above analysis of arguments, but this time for those previous stages that led to the premises themselves.
2. Certain premises may be assumed to be just self-evident. For example, the old metaphysical claim that 'nothing can come from nothing'. Also, in the examples in 'Using these arguments' above, the premise that 'God is defined as the creator' may appear not to need justification. Or again, in the second example from that section, 'to identify or point to the cause means to be able to single out the cause'. But, in all such cases, you need to test the supposed self-evidence by asking such questions as: 'What would be the implications if the premise were false?', 'Are there other plausible but less common ways of defining a key term?' A great deal of dubious philosophy can be hidden in apparently straightforward definitions!
3. The premises may ultimately be based upon empirical observations, and thus induction. For example, in the 'design argument' example: 'If something is not made, then it will not show a trace.' The empirical, quasi-scientific nature of this statement is reinforced by the additional idea, found in the original passage we were

analysing, that apparent traces will turn out to be
illusions on close inspection. Certainly, the premise that
follows ('Many things in nature show the trace') is
empirical. In such cases you need to ask, 'Where's the
evidence? How reliable or well-studied is the
phenomena? Are there alternative ways of concluding
on the basis of the evidence?'

4. If you decide a premise is probably not true, you then
need to ask what happens to the argument. Is the
whole argument lost, or can a part of it be salvaged?
Can a weaker version of the premise be considered true
(for example, 'some x . . .' instead of 'all x . . .'), and if
so, again, what happens to the argument? Finally, can
you think of good reasons for supporting the premise,
even if the author you are working on cannot? Can you
save his or her argument?

5. Don't forget to go through similar reflections on the
premises to your own arguments. That's part of being a
conscientious and honest philosopher.

6.1.1.8 Summary: what to do with arguments

If you are presented with the argument of a philosopher –
whether in a book you are reading for an essay, in a lecture, or
perhaps even an argument of your own – and wish to analyse
it, what do you do?

1. What is the conclusion? What is the philosopher trying
to show must be true?

2. Identify as many steps as possible in the argument.
Which of these are premises (that is, sentences that
we take to be true) and which are intermediate
stages (sentences derived from the premises). Don't
forget that you may have to weed out some
sentences that are simply irrelevant, that several mini-
arguments may be found in the same paragraph, and
that some steps may need to be interpretively
reformulated in order to make their logical
relationships to the others clear.

3. Try to think through the relation between the steps. What follows from what? Evaluate these relations using the rules given above. Are these relations valid?

4. Rewrite the argument in paraphrase making clear the steps you have identified, and also the relationship between them. This will help you to do the following:

   a. Now that you have pinpointed the premises, you need to enquire whether they are true. See section 6.1.1.7, 'Evaluating the premises', above.

   b. Consider what *else* must be true in order for the steps to lead inevitably to the conclusion. These will be *assumptions*. What are they? Are they true, or at least plausible? Why or why not?

   c. Define and explain key terms used in the argument as clearly as you can. Are there good reasons for agreeing with the way key terms are defined, or disagreeing?

   d. Think of additional examples or analogies to make things still clearer. Or perhaps counter-examples that raise questions about how the argument is viewing basic issues.

   e. Note any ambiguities or possible different interpretations in your paraphrase of the argument's steps. How does it change the argument if we interpret a key step in one way rather than another?

5. If the steps are valid, and the premises true, then the argument is sound. But where does this conclusion get us, or why is it important? What problems does it solve, illuminate – or perhaps does it raise new problems? Is it perhaps only one step in a larger argument?

6. If the argument is invalid, or some of the premises/assumptions false, is there any way that you can 'save' it? In general, when you are explicating or studying a philosopher, you have a *duty of generosity* to that philosopher. It would be a pity to throw out a potentially illuminating idea just because of a flaw in the argument that can be repaired. Maybe you can

save the argument by changing (often *weakening*) a premise, or the conclusion. If so, what impact does that have on the philosopher's overall position?

6.1.2 Examples and analogies

As part of an argument, examples can be used in four basic ways: empirical evidence, illustration, eidetic illustration, or hypothetical scenario.

First, examples from real life can be instances of a proposed general rule, and can thus count as *empirical evidence* for the validity of that rule. Thus, the example forms part of an inductive argument (see section 6.1.1.2, 'What kinds of argument are there?', above). If your claim was that 'wars tend to be followed by periods of economic growth', you might look to examples of historical wars and their aftermaths for evidence. Of course, you would have to be careful: no empirical generalisation is going to receive much credence based upon one or two examples; the examples have to be both true and accurately reported; and the examples cannot be specially selected to prove your point, but must be representative. The science of asking when empirical evidence is adequate to a certain degree of confidence in a conclusion is 'statistics'. Such a use of examples is unlikely to show up in a philosophy essay. We'll move on.

Second, and much more likely to be used in philosophy essays, an example can be an *illustration*. Suppose I am writing about how colours are perceived, and I talk about the perception of a certain shade of blue. The purpose of this example is to be a further explanation of my point. As such, the example doesn't supply any evidence for my conclusion (and thus doesn't help me to justify that conclusion) it merely helps to make more clear to the reader what I mean by my conclusion. So, beware of claiming that an illustrative example, or even a series of them, somehow proves your point.

Third, something we shall call the 'eidetic illustration'.

Here, just like in the second type of example, I am using the example to explain. But I also have another purpose. Consider Hume's example of an angry man (at the beginning of section II of the *Enquiries Concerning Human Understanding*): 'A man in a fit of anger, is actuated in a very different manner from one who only thinks of that emotion.' Such an example functions by pointing to a general rule, but also challenging the reader to agree that the truth of this rule is simply obvious. This would be an eidetic illustration. '*Eidos*' is Greek for 'idea'. Such an example is not meant to simply explain Hume's idea, but to verify it. In the example, the reader is supposed to not only see the idea more clearly, but to see the example as a genuine *representative for all possible examples*, and thus the idea *as undoubtedly true*. But be careful. It may be the particular example, rather than the general principle, that is obvious! The eidetic illustration functions as an argument only to the extent that a counter-example cannot be found; this would show that the original example truly is eidetic, rather than just fortuitous. But how could you rule out the possibility of any counter-example? Hume was a master of the use of eidetic illustrations, and this is one reason he is such an engaging writer, but also sometimes a slippery customer! In your own work, an example of this type is very unlikely to be considered 'justification' by your tutor. So, do not rely on eidetic illustrations on their own; back them up with careful analysis.

Fourth, the hypothetical scenario or thought-experiment. Suppose there were a time machine and you could travel forward in time. In the future, you commit a crime. Can you justly be prosecuted for it upon your return to the present, since the crime hasn't yet occurred? This fanciful scenario is designed to help us see, as clearly and purely as possible, something about the nature of time, justice or responsibility. It does so by magnifying or diminishing the role of one aspect of a problem, or by putting an idea to the test in an extravagant circumstance. The truth of the conclusion is based not upon the hypothesis (which clearly isn't true – yet, anyway!), but upon the analysis of time or justice that the scenario facilitates.

The scenario thus functions like an illustrative example, or perhaps even an eidetic illustration. Thus, as a justification it has the same limitations.

How do you test examples – that is, ask whether they are appropriate, or whether they help to make a point – whether in your own work, or some else's?

- Try to think of *counter-examples*. That is, a real or imagined instance in which the general rule would not hold. This is a good way of establishing whether or not an example is representative. Sometimes, though, counter-examples can be difficult to think of, not because the example has universal validity or is eidetic, but only because the assumptions it employs are so deeply engrained in everyday thought.

- Is the example too artificial or fanciful? Is perhaps the point much less clear in a more realistic example, and why might that be significant?

- Is the example being used as empirical evidence, and if so are we being told that *all* examples will be like this one, or only that most (or many) will be? (The latter conclusion is much easier.) How could it be demonstrated that the example(s) are genuinely representative? Clearly, it must be a real example. With illustrative and eidetic illustrations, though, the example could be entirely fictional.

- As a philosopher, you have duties of *discipline* and *generosity*. You should be hard on your own examples, in order to ensure that your essay's conclusion is as clear and well justified as it can be. You should be 'soft' on the examples of others, in order to ensure that their poorly chosen example is not masking a really interesting or important idea. You might consider whether you can think of a better example, or try to evaluate the validity of the underlying idea without the distracting example.

A few general points about the use of examples in your work:

- To summarise the above, the main purpose of examples in philosophy essays is to explain points, not to justify them.

- In your essay, you can fortify your position by showing why apparent counter-examples are actually not counter at all.

- Since their chief purpose will be to illustrate or explain, simple examples are always preferable to complex ones.

- In philosophy, only rarely should you try to find more than one example to illustrate a point. If you can think of two or more, just use the one that illustrates best. Only if, after your best efforts, you cannot alight on a single example that gets across your full meaning should you use two.

- Not every point you make in an essay may require an example. Put yourself in your reader's shoes: would you understand the point, on first encountering it, without the help of an example? Unnecessary examples can waste valuable space.

- Examples that you have found in primary or secondary literatures should be referenced just like anything else.

Analogies have a similar function to examples: that is, they are mainly devices for explaining an idea. Consider the following rather silly analogy:

Philosophy tutorials are like hunting parties, tracking down the big game of truth. If someone in the party doesn't contribute, or tries to obstruct the others, then the chances are the game will get away. Therefore, all the students in the tutorial should prepare and contribute to discussion.

An argument from analogy works by saying that two things are alike in many respects, therefore we have good reason to suspect that they are alike in further respects. Since the first half of the analogy has some further property, this permits the conclusion that the other half also has this same further property. Since the success of hunting parties relies upon every member of the party doing his or her bit, that must also be true of tutorial groups.

But more than likely the point here was not to *prove* the point about tutorial groups, as to suggest and illustrate an idea (*tutorial groups should work as a team*, or something like that). For, as a proof, the argument is open to plenty of objections. In general, just because two things have several features in common doesn't entail that they *must* have other features in common, or even that it is *probable* that they do. So, an analogy doesn't carry very much weight as evidence.

So, how do you deal with analogies in your own, or someone else's, work?

- If the analogy is being used as an argument, rather than just an illustration, it needs much more careful scrutiny. The two things compared in an analogy have to be *relevantly similar*. I could compare a tutorial group with the people sitting in the waiting room at the dentist's office, and conclude from this that philosophy students have bad teeth. In both cases you have people sitting in the same room. Well, so what? How is that relevant?

- The 'further property' must be *integral* to the things compared. Suppose I concluded that students in tutorial groups should carry rifles. That would be to allow my mental image of the hunting party to get lost in superficial details (in this case, the particular weapons employed). Such a detail is hardly integral to what is meant by a hunting party.

- As a philosopher, you have duties of *discipline* and *generosity*. You should be hard on your own analogies, in order to ensure that your essay's conclusion is as clear and well-justified as it can be. You should be 'soft' on the analogies of others, in order to ensure that their poorly constructed analogy is not misleading you into thinking that the underlying philosophy is also poor. You might consider whether you can think of a better analogy, or try to evaluate the idea without the aid of analogy at all.

The pointers for using analogies in your work are similar to examples: simplicity is best; normally use only one analogy per point, at most; perhaps an analogy is not needed and the idea is clear enough without it; borrowed analogies should be referenced.

6.2 WRITING CLEARLY AND CORRECTLY

6.2.1 References and bibliographies

A reference is the indication you give, for every borrowed idea or quotation in your essay, of its source. This is also called the 'citation'.

   The bibliography is a list, at the very end of the essay, of all the sources to which you have actually referred in the essay. (This is more properly called a list of 'Works cited', but we'll stick to university convention and call it a bibliography.) Thus, it is *not* a list of things that might have been relevant, things recommended to you, or even things you read but did not in fact employ.

   Every essay will have to provide both of these.

6.2.1.1 References

The purpose of references and bibliographies is to enable your readers to find for themselves the materials you have used. They may want to check your accuracy or, more positively, they may be stimulated by your writing to go and find out more. So, if in doubt, be sure to include sufficient information to enable this.

   Your university or department may prescribe the exact

format in which you must reference and write your bibliography. Follow it exactly, noting the order of information, and
the location of commas or full stops. On the other hand, a
format may not be prescribed. This does not mean that you do
not need to reference. It does mean that you need to pick a
system and stick to it consistently.

1. HARVARD SYSTEM

Whenever you are picking up another author's idea, even if you
are not using the exact words, you must reference the source.
There are two main systems for this. The easiest (called the
'Harvard' system) is to put the author's surname, the date of
publication and the page number in parentheses (Wiseman 1999:
911) after the citation. Or, if the author's name is part of your text,
just put the date and the page number in parentheses:

Wiseman (1999: 911) argues that . . .

If an author has more than one publication of the same date,
these are designated 1999a and 1999b and so on. Note that we
are talking about the publication date of the actual book you
used, not the original publication date of the text: so (Descartes 1640: 66) is probably wrong.

If the reference occurs at the end of a sentence, then it goes
inside that sentence's punctuation.

Wiseman argues that . . . (Wiseman 1999: 911).

Finally, in a complex sentence or passage, there might be
several ideas, some borrowed, some your own. Make sure you
make it clear which idea is being cited. You might be able to do
this by the location of the reference in the sentence; or you may
have to spell it out: 'Wiseman claims that . . . but I argue
that . . .'

2. NUMBERED NOTES SYSTEM (MLA SYSTEM)

The other system is to use foot- or endnotes. So, rather than
the information in backets, there will just be a number like so.[4]

Then, in the notes section, you would have something like the following:

4. A. Wiseman (1999), *Sense and Reference* (Chicago: Peacock University Press), p. 999.

Note that the book title is in italics (you could also have used underlining). Whether mentioned in the body of your essay, or listed in a bibliography, you must indicate book and periodical titles in this way. Articles within books or periodicals, however, are indicated by putting their titles in quotation marks.

If you use the same text for two consecutive references, then do the following:

5. Wiseman, ibid. p. 1003.

After having referenced to the full details (as in imaginary note 4 above), you can use a shorter form for further, but not consecutive, references. So:

8. A. Wiseman, *op.cit.* p. 998.

So, there are two general systems: the Harvard, and the numbered notes systems. Your department will either prescribe a system, or allow you to chose which of these you use, but don't use *both* in the same essay. All things being even, we recommend the Harvard system. The Harvard system is easier for the author to produce and manage while writing, and is easier for the reader trying to track a reference.

6.2.1.2 *Important note on plagiarism*

Proper referencing is essential if you are not to be accused of *plagiarism*.

Plagiarism, whether intentional or unintentional, is a form of cheating which universities are very concerned about and they are increasingly vigilant to ensure that students do not copy work from other students, from published sources or from the Internet. There are even computer programmes designed to detect plagiarism. Internet sources are a particular problem: there is a lot of material out there, and it is very tempting for students up against a deadline; of course, it's also very easy for tutors to find the source of a suspicious passage!

Naturally, you will present and discuss other people's ideas, opinions and theories in your essay, but you must say where you found them and you must be very careful not to claim them as your own original thoughts.

You will be heavily marked down, and probably failed, if you are found to be plagiarising. Books like this one emphasise the problem of plagiarism so strongly that there should no longer be any excuse. Students have even been expelled from university for this offence.

It's easy to avoid plagiarism, though. In addition to the above comments, follow this advice:

1. 'Other people's work' includes your fellow students' work, so be particularly careful that the work you turn in is your own when you have been working with a group. Sometimes of course you may have discussed your prospective essays as a group, but each member of the group should write their own notes on this discussion. Then, every word of the essay should have been written by *you* and from *your* notes. Probably you should indicate in the first foot- or endnote to the essay that the essay topic was discussed in a group setting, who was in the group, and when the discussion(s) took place. By the same token, you should not knowingly allow another student to copy part or all of your essay, or even to use your research notes.

2. *Everything you have used for your essay counts as a source, and requires a reference.* This includes assigned course textbooks, and general reference books (although neither of these tend to be good sources when it comes to essay writing). Most lecturers probably do not require you to cite their lectures, but some may, or the department may have a policy on this. In any case, if you have quoted directly from your

lecturer, or straightforwardly borrowed some idea or way of thinking about an idea, then a reference is probably a good idea. In the reference and bibliography, you should list the lecturer, and the title, date, time and location of the lecture.

3. When taking notes, be sure to make it clear to your later self what is your own idea, and what is someone else's. In the latter case, state exactly where it comes from, and whether it is an exact quote or your summary. Then, when writing, reference the sources as you go along.

4. Be sure to reference borrowed ideas, even if you've expressed them in your own words. To not do so is a very common mistake. 'Borrowed idea' is a broad concept. It includes factual information that is not common knowledge; distinctive philosophical concepts, distinctions, arguments or interpretations of these; methods, procedures or ways of analysing a problem; use of examples and their analysis. In brief, *any way in which a secondary text helped you is likely to require a reference.* The only notable exception is a source of a widely available piece of knowledge: the diameter of the Earth, the date of Newton's birth, the spelling of the word 'etymology'. However, if in doubt, stick in the reference.

5. Beware also the reverse mistake: paraphrasing a source, and thus supposedly using your own words, but in fact using a distinctive word or phrase from the source. By a 'distinctive word or phrase' is meant something that wouldn't be likely to be found in *anyone* writing on the topic. So, for example, anyone writing on Descartes would be likely to use the phrase 'philosophy of mind', but the phrase 'sovereign act of introspection' is probably distinctive, and you should indicate in your essay that it is a quotation.

6. On a related topic, you shouldn't expect to get credit for the same work twice. So, if you are taking two courses that happen to have set similar essay questions,

you will probably be strongly discouraged from writing on these similar questions. Also, one course might require both an essay and an exam. The exam may well contain specific instructions that you are not to write on the same topic as your essay.

6.2.1.3 Bibliographies

Bibliographies are a chore, but the task can be made a lot easier if you note all the necessary information right from the very beginning of your research. It is soul-destroying chasing round libraries looking for things like page numbers and place of publication when the rest of the job is done.

The perfectionist will ensure that the latest, updated editions of books are consulted, or perhaps the authoritative, 'standard' edition. Unless advised otherwise by your tutor, this shouldn't worry you too much. List in your bibliography the book that you actually referred to.

If you are referring to a website, you must make sure that you give enough information to make sure that a reader could access the same site. Give the date that you accessed the site, in case the site has been updated since then. With an Internet site, you should also travel up the hierarchy of the site in order to find out who produced it, and for what purpose.

The exact formats for bibliographies vary greatly and attention should be paid to where full stops, commas and so on are used. Again, your university/department may have a fixed style sheet. If there is no set format, the following is probably the most widely used. They are examples of the Harvard system for (respectively) a book, an article in a journal (or newspaper or magazine) and for an essay in a book.

Author, A. N. (1995), *Book Title in Italics*, 3rd edition, trans. S. Scribbler, Vol. 2 (Place: Publisher).

Wiseman, N. (1996c), 'Article title without capitals', *Italicised Journal Name*, 10.3, pp. 1–55.

Guilty, I. M. (1991), 'An essay in a book'. In S. Cribble (ed.), *Book Title* (Place: Publisher).

Notice that in the Harvard system, since your citations were identified by author and date, this information comes first in the bibliography.

These are examples for the numbered notes (MLA) system; don't get the systems confused!

Author, A. N., *Book Title in Italics*, 3rd edition, trans. S. Scribbler (Place: Publisher, date), Vol. 2.

Wiseman, N., 'Article title without capitals', *Italicised Journal Name*, 10.3, year, pp. 1–55.

Guilty, I. M., 'An essay in a book'. In S. Cribble (ed.), *Book Title* (Place: Publisher, date).

Journals come out in sets, usually annually, called 'volumes'. The individual issues within that volume (say, the 'Spring' issue) is called a 'number'. The '10.3' in the above refers to the tenth volume of the journal, and the third number in that volume.

Note that not every book will have as relevant information a volume number, an edition, or a translator. Further, note that for the journal, you should include the page numbers of the whole article, not just whatever pages you happen to have used.

Bibliographies are arranged alphabetically by the authors' names. Primary and secondary sources all go on the same list. If you are using more than one text by the same author, then they are arranged alphabetically by the title. Also, it is not necessary to write the author's name out each time. So, again using the Harvard system, you would write:

Guilty, I. M. (1991), 'An essay in a book'. In S. Cribble (ed.), *Book Title* (Place: Publisher).
  – (2001), 'An essay published on the internet'. *An Internet philosophy Journal*, 2.1. <www.poppy-

cock.edu/philosophy/journal/vol2/guilty.html>. (Cited 12 June 2002).
– (1989), Introduction to *A Very Fine Book* by S.
Else. (Place: Publisher).
– (1999), 'A most interesting article', *Famous Jour-*
nal, 16.1, pp. 31–42.

Note the indents and dash in the list of works by the same
author. Also note that titles are sorted alphabetically not by the
'A' or 'An' but by the first (and then second) 'real' word in the
title. Finally, notice the correct format for listing an Internet site,
and an introduction written to someone else's book.

Here are some other special case examples, all using the
Harvard system.

If the work you are citing is an encyclopedia, give the title of
the article prefaced by 's.v.'.

Eminent, I. M. (ed.) (2002), *The Self-Important Ency-*
clopaedia of philosophy (Place: Publisher), s.v.
'Descartes'.

If the encyclopedia makes a great show of who wrote that
particular entry, include that information: 's.v. "Descartes" by
A. Author'. Of course, if you are interested in the entry
because it is by a particular philosopher, then list the whole
thing under his or her name.

If it is an interview, list according to interviewee, but give
also the name of the interviewer.

Author, A. (1997c), 'Contemporary Issues in Descartes
Studies'. Interview by Guilty, I. In *Famous Journal*,
16.1, pp. 31–42.

If it is a review, list under the name of the reviewer.

Guilty, I. M. (2001), 'What a Rotten Book', review of
Book Title by A. Author. In *Famous Journal*, 16.1, pp.
31–42.

If it is an unpublished Ph.D. dissertation (yes, you can get these, they'll be lodged in the library of the university for which they were written), say so, along with the university at which the Ph.D. was granted.

> Author, A. (1978), *Juvenile Thoughts on Descartes*. Unpublished Ph.D. dissertation, Department of Philosophy, University of Poppycock.

If it is a paper read out at a conference, say so, giving also the title, date and location of the conference. Similarly, for a lecture that is part of your university degree.

> Eminent, I. M. (1999), 'A Two and a Half Hour Paper Read Very Quickly'. Unpublished conference paper for 'Thirst: A Conference of Academics Dying to Get to the Pub'. Delivered 12 July 1999, University of Poppycock.

> Tedious, V. R. (2003), 'Nineteen Objections to the First Sentence of Descartes' *Meditations*'. Unpublished lecture for 'PY110: Introduction to Metaphysics'. Delivered 2 March 2003, University of Poppycock.

Sometimes you'll need to cite one author who is in turn citing another. The reference would look like this: (Jones 1967, cited in Smith 1998: 23). The page number is the page in Smith. Full information on Jones' book would be included in your bibliography, but then you would add 'cited Smith 1998' to the entry. Smith's book would then also appear in the bibliography.

6.2.2 Good academic style

What follows is a brief guide to style for all your written work. The style you are aiming for is *not* the same as you will find in newspapers and magazines, or hear on radio or television.

Different types of writing have different purposes: to persuade, to inform, to entertain, to enrage and so forth. Philosophical writing at university has as its sole purpose achieving a justified answer to a question. That is, its purpose is ultimately the same as essay writing itself. Thus, every sentence you write should be subordinated to that purpose. Academic style is, to be frank, drier and more impersonal than most other forms. But it is also clearer, more precise, more patient, and thus ultimately more *powerful*. (Note: this book is written in a less formal style for the most part, but the sample essays and exam answers provided are about right.)

6.2.2.1 Paragraphs

A paragraph is the complete development of a relatively simple idea. Finish that, move on to the next idea – start a new paragraph. As such, a paragraph is only rarely shorter than three sentences. Too many such short paragraphs, and the reader starts losing the wood for the trees. Anything above ten sentences, though, and you should ask yourself if this is really one simple idea, and not two.

SIGNPOSTING

Your essay will be a complex thing made up of many different points. All the points are supposed to add up in some way so as to reach your conclusion. How does your reader know how your points add up? You tell them. 'Signposting' is the practice of making it clear to your reader where you are in your overall argument, and what you are up to next. So, for example, 'It is now clear that Descartes' argument relies upon an ambiguity in his use of the term "body". The next section of this essay will explore in greater detail the two different meanings of "body" that Descartes employs.'

TOPIC SENTENCES

You should have one topic or core idea per paragraph. It is a good idea to summarise it in a topic sentence. A topic sentence is a brief statement of what you intend to achieve in the paragraph. So, for example, 'In order to carry the argument further, it is essential to define what Descartes means by "imagination" '.

The best place for the topic sentence is at the beginning of the paragraph because it makes for easy reading if your reader knows what you are writing about. If your reader is scanning through your work, the first sentence of each paragraph will catch the eye. You can put it at the end, which is also a position which gives emphasis, but that makes it harder work for the reader. In longer and complex paragraphs, put a topic sentence at both beginning and end, with the sentence at the end also pointing forward to your next step.

As you write, keep your topic sentence in mind. When you find yourself straying from it, you should be on to the next paragraph. For an interesting variation, your topic sentence could take the form of a question: 'What does Descartes mean by "imagination", exactly?'

CONVERSATION

When you are writing, you are holding a conversation without being able to hear the other person. At the end of each paragraph, in a conversation, your partner would come in with a comment like:

> *Could you give me an example?*
> *You have given me a whole lot of examples. Are you going to infer something?*
> *Ah, but what if . . . ?*
> *Say that again another way. I didn't understand a word of it!*

If your paragraphs are well planned, the next paragraph should be a reply to the comment. So, if you try to write like one half of a conversation, the result should be clearer and a pleasure to read.

INFERENCE

In a real conversation, however, there is a lot of work being done on both sides. That is, there will be other verbal or nonverbal clues in the air, and other opportunities to establish meaning. For example, in conversation, you can give signals with your own facial expressions and other gestures, or you alter your tone of voice. Moreover, you can see if there is a bewildered or angry or approving expression on a hearer's face. You can even ask little 'tag' questions just to make sure the conversation is going as you intend. *Right?* If an appropriate, unambiguous inference cannot be made, your hearer can ask what you mean. *Can you say that again?* Unfortunately, in the act of writing, you are deprived of all these safety checks.

When you write as if it were one half of a conversation, you must realise that opportunities for the exchange of such signals will be missing. Thus, you must compensate by signposting and explaining more frequently. (This is doubly true for oral presentation.)

Similarly, you cannot assume that just because your reader is an expert in the subject, he or she will know what you mean anyway and reconstruct some sense from your half-expressed musings. And, even if your tutor *can* understand your meaning, you'll probably lose points for such musings – since, after all, part of the purpose of getting you to write essays is for you to prove that you can do rigorous, intelligent and complete philosophical work.

LINKING

In the best writing, one paragraph naturally and necessarily flows on to the next. Between paragraphs, take time to reflect:

- What did I establish in the last paragraph?

- How does my next paragraph relate to it?

In case the relationship is not immediately clear, it is helpful to have a few strategies ready to help you link paragraphs to each other.

For example, you could start with a paragraph that lists the topics to be discussed in the following paragraphs. You could end with a paragraph that summarises the preceding paragraphs. That may not be appropriate, if you are trying to follow an argument from beginning to end, in which case it might be helpful to have some signals ready to link paragraphs:

Enumerative: First . . . Second . . . Third . . . Finally . . .

Additive: Another example . . . Furthermore . . . Moreover . . .

Contrastive: By contrast . . . On the one hand . . . On the other hand . . . Alternatively . . .

Beware, however, of overusing any of these links as they can easily become intrusive and irritating. Watch your writing very carefully for links that are becoming too much of a habit. *However* is one that many people pepper their work with.

6.2.2.2 Sentences

The important thing about sentences is to keep the words in the right order. Do not alter the natural word order for rhetorical effect unless you really know what you are doing and you are sure that your meaning will be made more rather than less clear.

The subject of the sentence goes at the beginning. It is no accident that the grammatical 'subject', the one that 'does' the verb, goes before the verb. The subject is what the sentence is about and the rest of the sentence is saying something about the subject. The second most conspicuous position in a sentence is at the end. Occasionally, it can be effective to build up to a climax at the end of a sentence.

A sentence has to have a subject, and has to have a verb. Just has to. Otherwise it is a 'sentence fragment', and these are considered bad style. The words 'just has to' in this paragraph are a sentence fragment, and should be cut out in formal, academic writing.

A sentence is as long as it needs to be. If you are building complex relationships, your sentence might have to be very long, but if you keep the structure simple, a long sentence does not have to be difficult. Do not try to tuck too many additional bits of information into a sentence or your reader will loose the main thread. If you are having trouble navigating in your own sentence, that's a sign that it needs to be split in two. Too many short sentences sound rather ugly and fail to develop links and relationships, but the very occasional short, sharp sentence can give a dramatic emphasis. Try to give your reader a bit of variety of sentence length.

CASE AGREEMENT
By 'case agreement' is meant that a singular subject requires a singular verb, and a plural subject requires a plural verb. Two simple examples:

> *A person has duties.*
> *People have duties.*

Try swapping 'has' for 'have' in the above, and you will be able to hear the case disagreement. Sometimes, however, this is not so easy to hear. A typical problem occurs when you need a gendered pronoun for a singular subject.

> *A person has duties and only because of this do they have rights.*

That's wrong, but it is harder to hear. Notice that 'has' changed to 'have'. This is because 'they' is plural. So, what pronoun should be used? There have been experiments in creating a new singular and ungendered pronoun for such circumstances, notably 's/he'. However, these have not caught on. There are two solutions: either make 'person' into the plural 'people' and write

> *People have duties and only because of this do they have rights.*

But there will be instances in philosophical writing where the plural is just not appropriate. So, alternatively, use 'he or she'.

> *A person has duties and only because of this does he or she have rights.*

Your university or department may have a policy on this.

BE IMPERSONAL

It is normal practice to avoid 'I' or 'me'. Most of the time, you are writing about the truth, or at least a possible truth, and not just about your own opinion. So, under 'Topic sentences' above (see p. 192), the example was not 'In order to carry the argument further, *I should* define what Descartes means by "imagination".' Departments, and even individual lecturers, vary in their acceptance of the use of *I* in academic writing, but there is an increasing awareness outside universities that the use of the passive is a way of avoiding responsibility. 'The report could not be submitted before the meeting' actually means 'Oops, I missed the deadline.' So, you need to know when to take responsibility for your own actions and opinions. When you want to make it clear that you are voicing a purely personal opinion, *I* is not only appropriate but essential: *It might be thought that* . . should be: *I think* . . . (Not: *The author thinks* . . . or *We think* . . .)

BE ACTIVE

Using the passive is a way of avoiding the use of *I*, but there is so much of the passive in academic prose that it becomes wearisome. Therefore, avoid it if you can.

> *It has been suggested by Smith* . . . should perhaps be: *Smith has suggested* . . .

BE POSITIVE

Negatives can overstretch your readers' logical abilities:

There are no *conditions under which the machine will* not *operate.*

Instead, how about:

The machine will operate under all conditions.

BE BRIEF
Word limits take into account the number of words necessary to deal with the set topic. Using unnecessary words for padding out (or running over the word limit) does not make for a good essay or for pleasant reading. Your tutor may well write 'get on with it!' in the margin of your essay. By how much can you shorten these examples?

A feature of much of this research is the illustration of . . .
There is continued, ongoing research . . .
Basically, the true facts may be said to be as follows: an undue and excessive proliferation of redundant and unnecessary modifiers and other repetitious or fairly weak insertions add very little or nothing to the meaningful impact of the discourse.

BE CAREFUL!
Sometimes you can be too brief:

Elephants do not require additional protection from buffalo. (I didn't know the buffaloes were even offering!)

Make sure that what goes together stays together:

Rabbit wanted for child with lop ears. (Poor little kid!)

Sometimes you can say more than you intended:

The doctor said that he had never before seen this rare subcutaneous parasite in the flesh. (Get it out, get it out of me!)

Be careful when starting a sentence with an -*ing* word or an -*ed* word. Make sure that the -*ing* or -*ed* word really does relate to the subject of the sentence or you could end up with nonsense like

Walking down the main street, the parish church comes into view. (Does the church have nice legs?)
Covered in a warm travelling rug, the coach bore him off into the night. (The coach was warm, but what about the passenger?)

Avoid beginning a sentence with 'But' or 'And'. This is considered poor style in academic writing.

USING PRONOUNS
Whenever you use words like 'this' 'it' or 'that', make sure it is clear what the pronoun is referring to. If you don't do *that*, then the reader will be unable to follow your argument. After a long ramble, students often write, 'This means . . .' when it is not at all clear what 'this' was. Usually, the pronoun reference will not be clear in the following circumstances: (1) if the sentence containing the pronoun 'that' does not immediately follow the sentence containing the idea to which 'that' refers; (2) If there are several ideas to which 'that' might refer; (3) If you are using several pronouns at once (such as a 'that', a 'it' and a 'this'). Try to imagine yourself as the reader, who does not know in advance what you are writing about. Is it perfectly clear what refers to what?

WHICH and THAT
Although in some versions of the English language, these two words can be used interchangeably, it is still worth remarking on an important difference in meaning. Consider the difference in meaning between the following two sentences:
    Philosophy books that are French make no sense.
    Philosophy books, which are French, make no sense.
The first sentence has a defining clause in the middle, marked by 'that'. It 'defines' or 'restricts' the noun 'books' only to

those that are French. It is only French philosophy books that make no sense. The second sentence contains a non-defining clause that does not restrict the noun; *all* philosophy books make no sense – and *all* philosophy books are French too!

Use 'that' in sentences with a final clause *that* is vital for the overall meaning of the sentence because it defines precisely what is meant by the noun. Use a comma and 'which' in sentences with a final clause that is not really vital, *which* is just a clarifying, additional or incidental point. Or, in other words, if you can write 'by the way' or 'additionally', use the word 'which'. Two more examples:

> *Descartes published* Discourse on the Method *in 1637,* **which** was his first publication.
> *Descartes puts forward an account of the mind* **that** explains why we can imagine the whole material world being an illusion.

SPLIT INFINITIVES

A *split infinitive* is when an adverb appears in the middle of a verb in the infinitive. An infinitive is a verb with 'to', such as 'Our five-year mission is *to go* where no man has gone before'. Put a modifying adverb after the to, and you get 'Our five-year mission is *to boldly go* where no man has gone before.' This is one of the most famous split infinitives in modern culture. Avoid using split infinitives if possible as they are widely considered to be poor style. Instead, put the adverb after the verb: 'Our five-year mission is *to go boldly* where . . .'

6.2.2.3 Using quotations

Think about why you use quotations. (See also section 5.1.6 above 'Finding and using sources'.) First, because sometimes a philosopher you read will say things better, more clearly, more concisely than you could yourself. In such a case, putting the idea into your own words would be inefficient. Still, though, an essay is a lot more than a string of brilliant quotes; you need to show your understanding and ability to handle the material.

So if more than a quarter of your essay by word count is quotations, consider cutting down.

Second, because the exact wording used by a philosopher is important. You wouldn't expect to get very far by merely paraphrasing a poem if you were writing a literature essay; sometimes philosophy essays need that same careful attention to language.

Those are really the only good reasons. The only really bad reason to quote is that you cannot think of anything to say yourself.

QUOTATIONS IN SENTENCES

Quotations do not need a different font, font size or (heaven forbid!) colour of ink. Just carry on into the quotation with the same font, please.

Quotations will either be incorporated into one of your sentences (if relatively brief), or be set off separately (if relatively long). Here is an example of the former:

> When Descartes writes that his 'purpose there was not to provide a full treatment' (Descartes 1997: 6), what he means is that . . .

The idea is for the sentence to flow grammatically in and out of the quotation. Notice that there is no introducing comma in that example. There would be a comma had the sentence begun:

> Descartes writes, 'My purpose . . .'

When deciding what punctuation to use, just think about the sentence as a normal sentence, ignoring the quotation marks – that should help you to see how the sentence flows. Punctuate it accordingly. Notice also that because the second example begins quoting at the start of Descartes' sentence, it uses a capital letter. Where the quotation is a complete sentence, you have the option also of using a colon:

Here is Descartes reasoning: 'But what then am I? A thing that thinks . . .'

MAKING THE QUOTATION FIT YOUR SENTENCE

In order for the grammar of the quotation to work with your sentence, or for the meaning of ambiguous words to be made clear, it is permissible to insert a word or phrase in square brackets.

James asserts that 'the real meaning of the impulses, it [materialism] says, is something which has no emotional interest for us whatever' (James 2000: 34).

Similarly, you can quote from two different but closely connected passages of a text, indicating the skip with an ellipsis (. . .). This would allow you to leave out of the quotation some material that is irrelevant to your purposes. But the two passages have to flow grammatically together. Sometimes to make the passages link grammatically you will need to add some text in square brackets. For example:

Author (1991: 21) writes, 'Descartes' general point here . . . [is that] nothing can be known of extended substance other than . . .'

These ellipsis and square-bracket techniques should not be overused, otherwise you will be distorting the meaning of the author's words. Since distortion would also be a danger if too much of the original is left out, never remove more than a phrase, or a single sentence at most. Above all your duty is to not misrepresent what the author says or clearly means. If you need to distort the original to make it fit your sentence, then you should change *your* sentence.

LONGER QUOTATIONS

For a quotation longer than, say, three lines, do this:

A quotation longer than, say, three lines should be in a paragraph of its own, indented on both sides, single spaced, and without quotation marks, followed by the reference. Only for such indented quotes, you may decrease the font size two points, but that is not necessary. Also, you will sometimes see a recommendation to insert a blank line before and after the block quote. However, since you will be 1 ½ or double spacing your essay, including the lines before and after the block, this is not necessary. (Author 1991: 13)

But when should you employ longer quotations, and how should they be used?

First, it is *normally* better to put an author's thoughts into your own words (adding a reference to the author, of course!), than to stick a long quotation into your essay. The reason is that, after a long quotation, you are going to need to comment on it anyway to show your mastery of it. You are also opening yourself to the accusation that you are just padding out the word count with detail that doesn't help to answer the question. However, there are certainly times when longer quotes are necessary: (1) when you feel the need to draw attention to the exact way that a philosopher expresses herself; (2) when you are having to interpret a passage, and you want to provide evidence that an author really does hold the view you are attributing to him.

Second, to help the reader, it is always a good idea to introduce long quotations so as to give your reader an idea of why you are quoting, and what to look out for. For example, 'In the following quotation, notice how Descartes continually backs away from stating what must, for the reader, seem obvious:'

FURTHER PUNCTUATION ISSUES

Punctuating quotations is a matter of pedantic but nevertheless fiery disagreement. The following simple rules may not make everyone happy, but will at least make your writing universally clear. As always, if your department supplies different rules, use them instead.

Notice that in the block quote in the previous section above, the reference comes after the final punctuation (this is to indicate that the whole of the quotation is from the same source).

When the quote finishes *within* your sentence, the punctuation should be placed outside the final quotation mark. But, when the quote *finishes off* your sentence, then the punctuation is within the final quotations mark. So:

> *Wiseman claims that, 'Descartes' observations at this point are unsurpassed', but that overstates the case.*

But:

> *Wiseman asks the question: 'Are Descartes' observations at this point unsurpassed?'(Wiseman 1999: 300).*

Note also that in the last example, we have an additional full stop after the reference. Otherwise the reference would dangle between sentences.

Should you happen to be quoting poetry (perhaps in one of your philosophy and literature interdisciplinary courses), use a '/' mark to show line divisions. If quoting more than three lines, use a block quote, and show the line divisions by starting a new line.

6.2.2.4 *Vocabulary*
JARGON
One person's technical term is another's jargon. In choosing your words, keep your target reader constantly in mind. When you are writing for your tutors and lecturers, you should be able to show that you have understood the technical terms and can use them correctly and appropriately. Also, always define terms in a philosophical (not an everyday) manner.

BIG WORDS

Do not use big words where a little one will do the same job. If by *termination* you mean *end*, then use *end*. There is nothing to be gained by substituting *utilise* for *use*. There is a place for big words where they are the best ones to convey an accurate meaning, but they are not to be used unnecessarily for the sole purpose of sounding authoritative. Be especially self-disciplined about avoiding words whose meaning you are not completely sure about. Either consult a dictionary or use a word you know.

FORMALITY

You need to maintain a certain level of formality. In selecting short, commonly used words, you must avoid any slang terms and colloquialisms. You should also avoid contractions (e.g. *don't*)

PREMODIFIERS

The build-up of long, heavily premodified, fluency-impairing noun-phrases is a common failing in academic writing.

This could be rephrased:

Too many adjectives before a noun often impair the fluency of academic writing.

MORE VERBS

Verbs make your text bounce along. Nouns and adjectives and prepositional phrases describing nouns are solid and slow your reader down. If you can use more verbs and fewer adjectives and nouns, you will sound much less boring:

After expulsion of the breath by the lungs . . .
After the lungs expel the breath . . .

You can increase the proportion of verbs to nouns by rewriting phrases like

make an adjustment to > adjust
come to the conclusion > conclude

Other examples which can be shortened to a single verb
include:

arrive at a decision
make an examination of
conduct an investigation into

NUMBER WORDS AND DATES

In formal academic writing, do you write out 'fourteen' as a
word, or put in '14' as a number? The most common rule is to
use words for numbers equal to or below one hundred, and
numerals when greater.

He weighed 115 kilograms by the time he was sixteen.

Dates should normally be written out either as '11 June 1852'
or 'June 11th, 1852'. Whole centuries are indicated as follows:

The eighteenth century was a period of rapid scientific
progress.

EFFECT/AFFECT

An 'effect' (noun) is the result of some action ('Health Service
reforms are having no effect.'). To 'effect' (verb) is to produce
or accomplish something ('The studio effected various changes
to the film without the director's consent.'). That is, 'effect' has
something to do with *results*. To 'affect' (verb) is to be
influencing something ('The effectiveness of the reforms is
being affected by low staff morale.').

6.2.2.5 Common abbreviations

c.   (*circa*) approximately. It is normally used to indicate
             that a date is only approximate, as in *This house was*
             built in c. 1752.

cf.   (*confer*) compare. Often used when you are looking at one passage, and believe there is an interesting comparison to be made to another passage. So: *Descartes defines the term in this way in the* Second Meditation *(but cf.* Third Meditation, *p. 39).*

e.g.   (*exempli gratia*) for example. *Descartes makes this claim in several passages, e.g. in the* Third Meditation.

ed.   Editor. Used in a reference or bibliography to indicate that the named person is the editor of a book; if more than one editor, the plural is eds.

edn   Edition. Books once published may be revised or updated, and a new edition published. 'Edn' is used in a reference or bibliography to indicate which edition of a book you have used in your essay.

et al. (*et alii, aliae,* or *alia*) and others (that is, other people, other places and so forth). Commonly used when there are three or more authors or editors to an article or book. *A. Author, et al. (eds.).* Note that this should be done only in the second and subsequent reference. In the first, and in the bibliography, you must list *all* authors/editors/translators.

etc.   (*et cetera*) and so forth. To indicate that there is a sequence or list that could be continued. This particular abbreviation is chronically overused: don't be lazy and use 'etc.' as a substitute for typing things out!

f./ff. following. Used with page references. If the citation goes over a page then write *pp. 8f.* If the passage citated carries on for more than one page, write *pp. 8ff.*

ibid.   (*ibidem*) in the same place. Used in referencing, see page 185.

i.e.   (*id est*) that is. *Descartes is forced to concede the point, i.e. he now has to rethink the argument from the ground up.*

n.   note. Used to indicate the fact that you are quoting
            from an author's note or footnote. *p. 16n.*

op. cit.   (*opere citato*) from the work that has already been
            cited. See the section on referencing (see p. 195)

p./pp.   page, pages.

sic   thus. Suppose there is a misprint in the original you are
            quoting – you don't want to get accused of it, so you
            put [sic] in the quote immediately after the mistake.

s.v.   (*sub verbo*) under the word/ heading. Used to in-
            dicate, at the end of a reference, the source of a
            reference in a dictionary or encyclopedia: *s.v. 'trans-
            cendental'*.

trans.   Translator. Used in references and bibliographies to
            record the name of the translator.

vol.   Volume. Used in references and bibliographies; the
            plural is *vols*.

6.2.2.6 Rhetoric

Figures of speech are more likely to be found in writing where
the purpose is to persuade or entertain than in the dispassio-
nate prose of academic discourse. Thus, figures of speech
should be used sparingly but, so used, can liven up your
writing, get your points across forcefully, and even make
things clearer for your audience.

SIMILES AND METAPHORS

If you are going to use such figures, chose ones that are really
vivid. Also, if you describe a parasite as looking *like a
courgette seed*, you need to be sure your readers are readily
familiar with courgette seeds.

REPETITION

Usually, you go to quite a lot of effort to vary your sentence
structure. A deliberate repetition of a pattern can therefore
attract and hold the reader's attention.

  I came. I saw. I conquered.

Why do bears, wishes and Billy Goats Gruff always repetitively come in threes? The universality of the number three in folklore testifies to its power. Here is another triplet:

Some books are to be tasted, some to be swallowed whole and some few to be chewed and digested. (Francis Bacon)

Here, the third time comes with a little extra. This is repetition and variation. Good writers have always exploited this device. Think of repetition with variation as the delivery of some weakening punches followed by the knock-out blow.

Use the device of repetition too . . . repeatedly, however, and your reader will just sigh and go make a cup of tea.

RHETORICAL QUESTION
A rhetorical question is a question that is not expecting an answer – instead, it is there to make an assertion. For example: *What does Descartes think he's up to?* This really means: *Descartes' argument at this point doesn't make much sense.*

Rhetorical questions can be very irritating if overused.

CLIMAX
For maximum impact, make points in increasing order of importance so that the reader's interest grows to a peak. If you do it the other way round, the reader will be bored by mid-sentence. Similarly, always give your weakest examples or weakest arguments first and save the best for last.

Note: It's important to realise that politicians, and others who use rhetoric professionally, are not necessarily interested in getting their point across as clearly and openly as possible. Being deliberately ambiguous, or exaggerating a claim, are indeed rhetorical tools but *should not appear in a philosophy essay*. Similarly, hiding potential weaknesses in your arguments with rhetoric. Wherever possible, philosophical writing should communicate *transparently*.

6.2.2.7 *Punctuation*

Punctuation is not there for decoration but to help the reader. Too much punctuation can get in the way of fluent reading and if you put a piece of punctuation in the wrong place, it is obvious that you do not know what you are doing, whereas if you leave a piece of punctuation out it looks like a little typing error. The lazy student will therefore follow the maxim: when in doubt, leave it out, and even the skilful student will use punctuation economically.

CAPITALISATION

Proper names of things and people are always capitalised, as are the names of places and dates: 'Arthur Author is the Springfield Professor of Philosophy at the Metropolitan University, and he is the author of *In Pursuit of a Critical Metaphysics*. He will be speaking at the Metropolitan University Conference Centre on Tuesday, 16 July, on the topic of "Nietzsche as a critical philosopher".'

Note that book titles are capitalised (and italicised) throughout, except for prepositions and pronouns such as 'of' or 'a'. You may underline, instead of italicise, book titles.

FULL STOPS .

Between the capital letter that begins a sentence, and the full stop that ends it, there should be one, and only one, complete statement. That is, effectively, a definition of a sentence. A full stop is used to indicate the end of a sentence. It is also used in special circumstances in composing bibliography entries, for example, or in abbreviations.

COMMAS,

First of all, commas separate the items in a list. Note that, at the end of the list, there is no comma before the *and* in UK English. For example:

> *The colours of the rainbow are red, orange, yellow, green, blue, indigo and violet.*

This includes lists of modifying words, such as:

*The last, most complex and strongest argument begins in
§11.*

Second, commas separate out non-essential bits in the structure of a sentence (in the following, what is essential is in upper
case):

Suddenly, THE DOOR SLAMMED.
After the door slammed, THE MAID SCREAMED.
*Meanwhile, back at the ranch, TONTO WAS, with great
skill, MAKING PANCAKES.*

Now, by 'essential' here is not meant what is essential to your
meaning. If you were a mystery writer, for example, it might
be extremely important indeed that the maid should scream
after the door slammed. By essential is meant that which forms
a complete, simple sentence on its own. (Just read the upper
case bits on their own, and you'll see they are brief, complete
sentences.)

Note how commas can change meaning. Compare

*The chainsaw jugglers, who had been drinking before the
show, beheaded themselves.*

with

*The chainsaw jugglers who had been drinking before the
show beheaded themselves.*

In the first sentence, the bit in commas is a non-essential
extra. Take it out and it's clear that *all* the jugglers lost their
heads. In the second sentence, though, there is no non-
essential information: *only* the drinking jugglers were
beheaded. Accordingly, think about the effect of adding
commas to:

The students who are good at punctuation do well in their essays.

If a section separated out by commas is, as in the last few examples, in the middle of the sentence, make sure your commas come in pairs. In the Tonto sentence above, there are two pairs of commas.

PARENTHESES ( )
Parentheses (often mistakenly called 'brackets') are used in the same way as a pair of commas.

The chainsaw jugglers (who had been drinking before the show) beheaded themselves.

In simple sentences, you are better off with commas. Parentheses are to be preferred to commas in longer or more complex sentences, where there might already be a pair or two of commas.

SQUARE BRACKETS [ ]
Square brackets are used when you need to make some type of comment in the middle of a quotation. For example, if you need to add a word to make the quotation grammatical. Please see 'Quotations in sentences' (p. 201).

DASHES –
Dashes can be used in pairs in much the same way as commas and parentheses, for sectioning off an optional extra. Again, it is probably best to use commas as a first resort, and only turn to parentheses or dashes if the sentence structure is getting too complicated. A single dash can also be used, but only rarely, to hang an extra phrase on to the end of sentences. In that case, the dash signals a long pause, much like a semicolon (see 'Semicolons' below); and thus you may as well use a semicolon.

Parentheses and dashes can be useful if pairs of commas start accumulating, and nesting inside one another. Compare

Bad writers, who frequently compose long-winded sentences, rendered, as this example shows, incomprehensible, more or less, to the average or even skilled reader, by the interpolation of little, badly positioned, extra bits, should be ostracised by the academic community.

with

Bad writers (who frequently compose long-winded sentences, rendered – as this example shows – incomprehensible to the average, or even skilled reader, by the interpolation of little, badly positioned, extra bits) should be ostracised by the academic community.

The second version is still dreadful, but not quite so nightmarish as the first!

SEMICOLONS;
If you feel that two sentences are so closely linked that you want to draw attention to the fact, you can use a semicolon instead of a full stop. For example:

The students got very high marks; nothing in their answers was irrelevant to the question.

Had these been two separate sentences, it would not be so clear that the second part was meant to be an explanation or account of the first.

Semicolons are also useful for lists where the individual items consist of more than one word, and especially if the individual items themselves contain commas:

I shared a flat with three exotic dancers from a Paris nightclub; a large, brown rat, which snored; a highly intelligent, but eccentric, philosophy student called Alfie, who had a pet snake called Lucy; an ex-politician; and several cockroaches.

COLONS :
Colons are used to introduce the following: (1) lists (as in this sentence), (2) examples or explanations as in the following:

Descartes has only one concern in this passage: to avoid falling into error.

Finally (3), to introduce quotations, especially when no verb of saying is present.

The Mayor began: 'Ladies and gentlement, this is indeed a historic night . . .'

If there is a 'verb of saying' (said, shouted etc.), you would normally just use a comma. For example:

The Mayor said, 'Ladies and Gentlemen . . .

See also 'Quotations in sentences' (p. 201).

Note that although colons and semicolons look rather alike, they are used for quite different purposes. Get them confused, and you risk confusing and annoying your tutor.

EXCLAMATION MARKS !
Avoid them. They have very little place in academic discourse. Certainly do not use more than one at a time.

QUESTION MARKS ?
Surprise: they come after questions. But as with exclamation points, don't use more than one.

HYPHENS -
These can be useful for resolving ambiguities. Consider the difference between

extra-marital sex and *extra, marital sex.*

Hyphens should also be used to avoid awkward spellings: *de-ice* rather than *deice* and *go-between* rather than *gobetween.*

If you are not sure whether a compound word is hyphenated or not, and you cannot find it in your dictionary, make a decision and stick to it.

QUOTATION MARKS ' '
Use quotation marks for quotes that are not offset into a paragraph of their own. You should also use quotation marks when you are talking about a word, rather than using it. For example.

> *The word 'spiritual' has a revealing etymology.*

It is conventional to use single quotation marks in all instances. However, if there is a quote within a quote, switch to double quotes for the inner quotation so that it is clear where the various bits begin and end. So:

> *Author (1992: 22) claims that 'when Descartes says that "I do not differ from the Angelic Doctor in any respect" he is referring to . . .'*

Quotation marks are misused in four main ways. First, to use a word ironically, with a sneer, or just because you not sure about something:

> *We should all start living in the 'real' world.*

Second, for inappropriate words. By the latter is meant a word that is inconsistent with the level of formality or precision you are using. If you think a word is not quite consistent with your formality level, find the proper word instead. For example,

> *The whole elaborate construction of the theory cannot disguise the fact that it is a 'dud'.*

Third, for emphasis. If you feel it is necessary to stress a word, underline or italicise it instead.

ELLIPSIS . . .

An ellipsis (. . .) shows that a portion of text has been omitted. See the examples in the section on quotation above. Note that normally you should only use an ellipsis for text missing in the middle of a quote, not at the beginning or end. In the examples in this book that use such an ellipsis (as in the entry under 'Quotation marks' above), this indicates that the example continues but that it is irrelevant. This is not something you will need to do in your essays! Also, don't use an ellipsis as a 'trailing off' effect at the end of a sentence, as a sign of your supposedly sophisticated irony, or in an attempt to be thought-provoking. In academic writing that just looks a bit, well, childish.

APOSTROPHES '

Apostrophes are the punctuation marks that people seem to find hardest. In fact, they are really easy. There are only three things to remember.

1. In formal writing, you will not use shortened words. So, use *do not* instead of *don't*; *it is* instead of *it's*; *is not* instead of *isn't*.
2. You do not need an apostrophe for a plural, unless it is a possessive.
3. Apostrophes are also used to show possession. These are the basic rules:
   If the possessor is singular, use 's (*The queen's crown*)
   If the possessor (singular or plural or a proper name) ends in -s, use ' (*Charles Dickens' novel; the rebus' solution; cats' tails*). (It is a common mistake to write *Charles Dicken's novel*, which apparently refers to a less well-known author by the name of Mr Dicken.)
   If the possessor is plural and does not end in -s, use 's (*men's heads, the media's morals*)
   In other words, make the plural first and the possessive after it.

The above rules are not without controversy. Your tutor may well want you to use 's on proper names (*Thomas's book*), and singular nouns ending in -s (*the rebus's solution*). Follow guidance if it is there, and be consistent.

If the possessor is indicated by a pronoun, do not use an apostrophe. You would never dream of writing his's, would you? The same goes for *its*. *His head*. *Its tail*. If you write *it's* that means *it is*.

When using two or more possessive nouns together, only the last has a possessive apostrophe. For example, 'Brown and Black's views on this issue, in their book *Philosophical Views*, is that . . .' If the names are not actually partners, it is better to write: 'The views of Plato and Aristotle on this issue are very different'. You do not need an apostrophe when using a genitive phrase (that is, a phrase with 'of' that indicates possession). For example, 'Kant and Hume's philosophies . . .' is correct, but 'The philosophies' of Kant and Hume' is completely incorrect. In the latter case, the genitive 'of' does the job of indicating possession, so it should just be 'The philosophies of Kant and Hume'.

This is not all that there is to say about punctuation, but it might be enough to prevent the commonest errors. When checking your punctuation, the question to ask yourself is always, 'Does it help the reader?

6.3 RECOMMENDED READING

In addition to a good dictionary and thesaurus, you might like to invest in one or two of the following, or find them in the library:

Hart's Rules for Compositors and Readers at the University Press, Oxford 39th edn, Oxford University Press. A compact manual with all you will ever need to know about abbreviations, capitals, hyphens, italics, numerals, quotations, symbols, foreign phrases and so on. It also has widely used proofreading symbols. Every professional academic writer should have one on his or her desk.

G. J. Fairburn and C. Winch get down to detail in *Reading, Writing and Reasoning*. (Buckingham: Open University Press, 1996). This is an excellent book.

J. Peck and M. Coyle provide help with the mechanics of writing in *The Student's Guide to Writing: Spelling, Punctuation and Grammar* (Basingstoke: Macmillan, 1999).

Philip Gaskell combines a useful summary of the basics of good writing with some well chosen examples of different styles in *Standard Written English* (Edinburgh: Edinburgh University Press, 1998).

R. Quirk and S. Greenbaum's *A University Grammar of English* (Harlow: Longman, 1973) A useful book to refer to on occasion.

Gordon Harvey's *Writing with Sources* (Indianapolis: Hackett, 1998). A brief, inexpensive and useful first guide to the mechanics of academic writing.

6.4 WRITING SKILLS SELF-ASSESSMENT

When you have completed a piece of work – and also when you get a marked essay back from your tutor – measure it up on the table below. Note down your strengths and weaknesses. Now and again when you write, look back on your comments on earlier work. Have you taken your own criticisms on board? Do certain weaknesses show up again and again? Find a way to solve them. Start with the books above; there may be writing skills courses at your university.

Constructive Comments

First impression:
  Layout
  Word processing
  Attention to detail

Content:
  Definitions
  Adequate research
  Argumentation
  Evaluation
  Balance of argument
  Fairness of presentation
  Answering the question
  Overall integrity of structure

Paragraphs:
  Length
  Signposting
  Conversation
  Linking

Sentences:
  Length
  Clarity
  Grammar (any particular issues?)

Vocabulary:
  Consistent formality
  Accuracy
  Clarity

Spelling:

Punctuation:
  Accuracy
  Helpfulness

Other comments:

INDEX